BLUE GUIDE

Literary Companion

LONDON

Compiled by
Robin Saikia

Somerset Books • London

Blue Guide Literary Companion London
First edition 2011

Published by Blue Guides Limited, a Somerset Books Company
Winchester House, Deane Gate Ave, Taunton, Somerset TA1 2UH
www.blueguides.com
'Blue Guide' is a registered trade mark.

The copyright acknowledgements appearing on p. 288 form a
part of this copyright page. All other in-copyright material
© Blue Guides Limited 2011.

ISBN 978-1-905131-44-0

A CIP catalogue record of this book is available
from the British Library

Distributed in the United States of America by WW Norton and
Company, Inc. of 500 Fifth Avenue, New York, NY 10110

Compiled by Robin Saikia
Edited and with additions by Annabel Barber
Image research by Hadley Kincade
Cover design by Anikó Kuzmich
Page design by Anikó Kuzmich, Blue Guides.

Printed and bound in Hungary by Pauker Nyomdaipari Kft.

CONTENTS

INTRODUCTION

This book is divided into chapters which reflect my view of London, a city I have lived in, loved and hated, for most of my adult life. By way of introduction, let me summarise what the chapters contain and the thinking behind them, in order to prepare the reader for an exploration of familiar and unfamiliar pieces, gathered together in what I hope is an unusual and effective sequence.

'London Visions' is a personal selection of pieces intended to give a feel of London's townscape over the centuries, what distinguishes it and what aspects might have changed for better or for worse. 'A Little Learning' touches on the troubled subject of education, while 'The Literary Life' dwells on two problems writers have always had, namely the necessity of doing something unpleasant in order to make money and the temptations that draw them away from potentially profitable commitments. 'Hard Up' examines the plight of the city's poor and their schemes for earning, borrowing or stealing money. 'At Home' takes us into the domestic sphere, where things are not always as comfortable as they seem, and 'On the Streets' rejoins the waifs and strays that populate the English capital. 'Addiction' illustrates the obvious point that games of chance are played as

Facing page: Ludgate Hill by Gustave Doré (1872).

much in the gutter (Alexander Baron) as they are among the stars (James Bond). 'War' examines personal attitudes to conflict rather than its physical consequences.

'Lions and Tigers, Cats and Dogs' celebrates London's ancient and thriving animal community. 'Dandies' is, if nothing else, an impassioned piece of advocacy for Savile Row tailoring. Some of the unpleasantness in 'Crime and Punishment' is offset by a sample from a fictional mystery thriller. 'Fire and Plague' brings together three great London writers: John Evelyn, Samuel Pepys and Daniel Defoe. 'Death, Burial and Beyond' explores what might be termed the London way of death, offering some intriguing possibilities as to a London afterlife, suggested by Henry Fielding, Emanuel Swedenborg and Bram Stoker. The collection ends with a poem by James Elroy Flecker that, to my thinking, sums up all that is good and bad in London life.

There are omissions, many—but this merely serves to underline the encouraging fact that there will always be room for further literary companions to London. The late Peter Vansittart, a sample of whose work appears in this book, published a wonderful companion to London in 1992. His guiding principle was to entertain rather than to instruct. That has been my approach too, though the somewhat dark chapter headings might appear to tell a different story. At all events, impassioned or purposefully written literature should never fail to do both.

Robin Saikia

LONDON VISIONS

Dorothy Wordsworth (1771–1855) was described by Coleridge as Wordsworth's 'exquisite' sister. Adored by her brother, she acted as muse, companion, friend and kindred spirit. She accompanied him to London in 1802 (when he wrote the famous sonnet reproduced here) and reports on the weather conditions they encountered that day. William Wordsworth (1770–1850) visited London often and was an enthusiastic, if outwardly taciturn, presence at literary and political meetings, parties and debates. His attendance at Benjamin Robert Haydon's 'Immortal Evening', when he met Keats, is recorded on p. 97.

Lord Alfred Douglas (1870–1945), known as 'Bosie', has a markedly different view of London from Wordsworth's, seeing the city as an abandoned debutante, glittering street lamps and illuminated houses her necklaces and tiara. Nowadays Bosie is remembered as the lover of Oscar Wilde and the son of the 'Screaming Scarlet Marquess', John Sholto Douglas, 9th Marquess of Queensberry. But he was an accomplished sonneteer, as his striking vision of London demonstrates. To the very end he believed that the moderns—T.S. Eliot, Ezra Pound, Edith Sitwell and the rest—were overrated and that *The Complete Poems of Lord Alfred Douglas* (1928) was the last word in poetry. In old age he lived in Hove in Sussex where a number of friends would take it in turns to wheel him to and fro on the promenade in his bath chair. One of these was Inez Waugh, later to become the first wife of the historian Christopher Hill. 'And who, would you say, is the greatest master of the sonnet in this or any tongue?' he memorably asked on one of these excursions, his words cut by the icy wind from the Channel, his resolute gaze still bearing the remains of his terrible beauty even in old age. 'Well I'm sure I don't know,' replied Miss Waugh, 'Shakespeare, perhaps?'

Amy Lowell (1874–1925) memorably describes London's 'plum-coloured night'. Lowell, an American poet, critic and lecturer, was born in Brookline, Massachusetts into one of the most respected and ancient of the Boston families. As well as producing an impressive body of poetry, prose and criticism she did much to help other writers, using her money, influence and considerable energy to great advantage. She met Ezra Pound in London when he asked permission to include her poem 'In a Garden' in his anthology *Des Imagistes* (1914). Her biography of John Keats (1925) was the first book to show Keats's fiancée, Fanny Brawne, in a favourable light.

Peter Vansittart (1920–2008) was a prolific author who in a distinguished literary career wrote 50 novels in addition to a wide range of historical studies, memoirs and anthologies, including a literary companion to London. The extract here is from his alternately disturbing and entertaining novel *Landlord*, based on his own experiences letting rooms in a house in Hampstead which he bought for £200 in the 1940s from a friend in the pub. Here Vansittart evokes the palpable sense of history, not all of it pleasant, that one picks up while wandering through London streets.

Henry Mayhew (1812–87), liberated for an interlude from his hectic career as a social historian and reformer, soars above London in a hot air balloon on a fine autumn evening. Mayhew was best known for his *London Labour and the London Poor* (2 vols 1851; reissued with additions 1861, 1862, 1864, 1865). It remains the most comprehensive first-hand study of London street life of the period, and his classification of the London criminal underworld (*see p. 222*) is a masterpiece of research.

Joseph Conrad (born Józef Teodor Konrad Korzeniowski; 1857–1924) began life as a master mariner, a background that provided many of the experiences he subsequently put to use in his later career as an author. On the publication of his first novel, *Almayer's Folly*, *The Spectator* prophesied that he might become 'the Kipling of the Malay Archipelago'. He became much more than that, producing a series of novels that deal with enormous themes such as isolation, solidarity, romantic aspiration, racial prejudice and the shadowy territory marked out between loyalty and treachery. The critic

Edward Garnett said of him, 'I had never seen before a man so masculinely keen yet so femininely sensitive'. His descriptions of London's docks in *The Mirror of the Sea* far outstrip those of many of his contemporaries and the short passage extracted here is a good example of how Conrad evokes time, place and atmosphere using economical and carefully judged description.

G.K. Chesterton (1874–1936) is represented by a striking poem in which he speculates how generations far in the future might react to Kings Cross Station. What was it for? Was it a place of worship? A powerful and effective poet, not easily classifiable as part of a movement, Chesterton was a devout Roman Catholic and wrote passionately in defence and explanation of his belief.

For centuries a persistent feature of the London cityscape was the 'smog', a thick mix of man-made smoke and natural fog. Today it has given way to a less visible but probably infinitely more malevolent pall of pollution in the upper atmosphere, but until well into the 20th century low-hanging smog was a defining feature of London. The following extracts reveal mixed feelings but many authors seem to relish the dusky aesthetic appeal of the periodically darkened city. There are clear days among these extracts too, where sunshine and clarity of light are warmly celebrated.

Byron's London is depicted as a 'wilderness of steeples' rising through a 'sea-coal canopy', a vision no longer to be seen except in paintings. The view from Parliament Hill today, by contrast, offers a depressing prospect of monster set-pieces by leading architects amid a cluster of baleful commercial new-build, St Paul's Cathedral just about visible in the thick of it and, on a good day, the fairground attraction that is the London Eye. An extract from the famous 'Guildhall' speech given by H.R.H. The Prince of Wales in 1987 deplores the extent to which four decades of post-war building frenzy has changed the London skyline forever.

D.H. Lawrence (1885–1930) is remembered primarily for the scandal surrounding the publication of *Lady Chatterley's Lover*, though controversy dogged him steadily throughout his life, partly as a result of his pacifist views. In March 1915, when he had finished *The Rainbow*, he remarked, with famous hubris: 'Now off and away to find the pots of gold at its feet'. The reviews were mixed, one of the opinion that 'A thing like *The Rainbow* has no right to exist in the wind of war'. His poems are striking and have stood the test of time well, partly because they were fortunate enough to escape easy categorisation: he arrived on the scene too late to be grouped with the poets of the Nineties; he was a pacifist and did not fight alongside Sassoon, Owen and the others; he was of too idiosyncratic a stamp to be grouped with the Georgians or with the Modernists. He offers a deathly image of the city, shrouded and corroded but nonetheless gleaming with a spectral beauty.

At times in 19th-century literature, London's fog can be too pervasive a presence. Oscar Wilde playfully suggested that the Impressionist painters were to blame for the 'wonderful brown fogs', and that 'people see fogs, not because there are fogs, but because poets and painters have taught them the mysterious loveliness of such effects'. In the shimmering dawn scene of Wilde's own *Lord Arthur Savile's Crime*, fog is completely absent. The story is a playful mystery in which the hero ludicrously (and unsuccessfully) embarks on a murderous scheme to remove the obstacles standing between him and marriage to the woman he loves.

John Evelyn (1620–1706) is noted for his extensive *Diary*, an invaluable account of life in London under Charles II. As many of his diary entries show, he was a close and valued confidant of the king, who tasked Evelyn with an investigation of the smog problem, to be put before Parliament. His *Fumifugium* (1661) was the first English book devoted to pollution and the extract reproduced here describes in robust terms the evils of unchecked smoke emissions and their long-term consequences. Evelyn served on numerous committees, all of them set up as part of Charles II's vigorous drive to improve the quality of life in London. His most important civic work was in planning the reform and expansion of the city's streets (1662–64), repairing St Paul's Cathedral (1666) and replanning London after the Great Fire (1667).

The American author William Dean Howells, a committed anglophile, offers an affectionate tribute to London fog, likening it to the excellent and equally atmospheric fogs he grew up with in Ohio. Another visitor, the German traveller Karl Moritz, describes how the city reveals itself when the air clears.

The extract from a poem by William Morris (1834–96) affirms the belief, held by him and his followers, that a bygone age was a better age, though it is doubtful if there ever really was a 'London small, and white, and clean' that conformed to this idealised vision. Morris was born in Walthamstow and enjoyed a successful career as a designer and author, his wallpapers and fabrics remaining popular to this day. It was inevitable that his commercial prosperity should come into conflict with his intense credo as a visionary socialist. On one occasion, when engaged in decorating Rounton Grange, the house of one of his principal clients, the northern ironmaster Sir Isaac Lowthian Bell, he lost his temper and stormed through the house crying 'I spend my life ministering to the swinish luxury of the rich.' Morris translated much of Virgil's *Aeneid* while travelling on the London Underground—an irony given his loathing for mechanisation.

The selection concludes with a nocturne by Oscar Wilde, at the end of which the reader is left in the presence of a solitary woman beneath a streetlamp, her 'lips of flame and heart of stone'.

Dorothy Wordsworth on a London morning

It was a beautiful morning. The city, St Paul's, with the river, and a multitude of little boats, made a most beautiful sight as we crossed Westminster Bridge. The houses were not overhung by their cloud of smoke, and they were spread out endlessly, yet the sun shone so brightly, with such a fierce light; that there was something like the purity of one of nature's own grand spectacles.

From the *Journal*, 31st July 1802

William Wordsworth: *Composed upon Westminster Bridge, September 3, 1802*

Earth hath not anything to show more fair:
Dull would he be of soul who could pass by
A sight so touching in its majesty:
This City now doth, like a garment, wear
The beauty of the morning; silent, bare,
Ships, towers, domes, theatres and temples lie
Open unto the fields, and to the sky;
All bright and glittering in the smokeless air.

Never did sun more beautifully steep
In his first splendour, valley, rock, or hill;
Ne'er saw I, never felt, a calm so deep!
The river glideth at his own sweet will:
Dear God! The very houses seem asleep;
And all that mighty heart is lying still!

Lord Alfred Douglas: *Impression de Nuit: London* (1909)

    See what a mass of gems the city wears
    Upon her broad live bosom! row on row
    Rubies and emeralds and amethysts glow.
    See! that huge circle like a necklace, stares
    With thousands of bold eyes to heaven, and dares
    The golden stars to dim the lamps below,
    And in the mirror of the mire I know
    The moon has left her image unawares.
    That's the great town at night: I see her breasts,
    Pricked out with lamps they stand like
                     huge black towers.
    I think they move! I hear her panting breath.
    And that's her head where the tiara rests.
    And in her brain, through lanes as dark as death,
    Men creep like thoughts... The lamps are like
                     pale flowers.

Oscar Wilde on dawn in London

    Where he went he hardly knew. He had a dim memory of wandering through a labyrinth of sordid houses, of being lost in a giant web of sombre streets, and it was bright dawn when he found himself at last in Piccadilly Circus. As he strolled home towards Belgrave Square, he met the great waggons on their way to Covent Garden. The white-smocked carters, with their pleasant sunburnt faces and coarse curly hair, strode sturdily on, cracking their whips, and calling out now and then to each other; on the back of a huge grey horse, the leader of a jangling team, sat a chubby boy, with a bunch of primroses in his battered hat, keeping tight hold of the mane with his little hands, and laughing; and the great piles of vegetables looked like masses of jade against the morning sky, like masses of green jade against the pink petals of some marvellous rose. Lord Arthur felt curiously affected, he could not tell why. There was something in the dawn's delicate loveliness that seemed to him inexpressibly pathetic, and he thought of all the days that break in beauty, and that set in storm. These rustics, too, with their rough, good-humoured voices, and their nonchalant ways, what a strange London they saw! A London free from the sin of night and the smoke of day, a pallid, ghost-like city, a desolate town of tombs! He wondered what they thought of it, and whether they knew anything of its splendour and its shame, of its fierce, fiery-coloured joys, and its horrible hunger, of all it makes and mars from morn to eve. Probably it was to them merely a mart where they brought their fruits to sell, and where they tarried for a few hours at most, leaving the streets still silent, the houses still asleep. It gave him pleasure to watch them as they went by. Rude as they were, with their heavy, hobnailed shoes, and their awkward gait, they brought a little of a ready with them. He felt that they had lived

with Nature, and that she had taught them peace. He
envied them all that they did not know. By the time he
had reached Belgrave Square the sky was a faint blue,
and the birds were beginning to twitter in the gardens.

From *Lord Arthur Savile's Crime*, 1891

Amy Lowell: *A London Thoroughfare, 2a.m.*

They have watered the street,
It shines in the glare of lamps,
Cold, white lamps,
And lies
Like a slow-moving river,
Barred with silver and black.
Cabs go down it,
One,
And then another.
Between them I hear the shuffling of feet.
Tramps doze on the window-ledges,
Night-walkers pass along the sidewalks.
The city is squalid and sinister,
With the silver-barred street in the midst,
Slow-moving,
A river leading nowhere.

Opposite my window,
The moon cuts,
Clear and round,
Through the plum-coloured night.

She cannot light the city;
It is too bright.
It has white lamps,
And glitters coldly.

I stand in the window and watch the moon.
She is thin and lustreless,
But I love her.
I know the moon,
And this is an alien city.

Peter Vansittart on a hot day in London

Deeper into London. The heat like blades working
from a cracked sky. Some clouds starting. Thundery.
Debbie had talked of lost countrysides and here gardens had dwindled to window-boxes and pots, and
leafy squares were locked to keep you out. Perhaps
a TV scene soon, presenting the last sheep in England quietly cropping, sightseers staring, pawing as
if for its autograph before the glaring cameras made
it whimper and panic. Eagles and vultures dead under the earth, ravens still lasting out in the Tower, tiger's bones dug from the Thames mud. Like the blue
whale, shattered for oil and corsets.

Outside a coffee-bar, stroking a sunshade, a bald
man whispered to a youth with over-red lips. Figures
sprawled inside, hair like shawls wrapped about soft
eyes. A young man with a pink nose sat very still,

white coat on his arm. Then the armoured car of
some security lot clanged wildly through the treacly
afternoon into which damp, weary plodders seemed
to squeeze.

She was always unexpected. She'd rested against
him. 'You're kind,' she'd said, but perhaps as a weapon
against love. Gratitude spoils sex, Edmund had once
told him, it's a drastic condom. At another time she'd
thrown in a surprise. 'I said to myself, "Bron thinks I
matter".' Then went overcast, distant, a hostile speck.

Love's picked up like an apple, heard like a song:
its quietness resounds, its tantrums soothe. In its gaze
the Alps become pebbles, bombs drop from a mis-
understood telephone call and saints are made from
false rumours and Tom Thumb's a giant at full stretch.
Nobody's still. Time jumps back to childhood, five
minutes are an hour, an hour's a desert, every instant's
a happening, the air can show talons, and flames
shine without light.

St Paul's now rising, a sunlit brain. Here too were
fields and hamlets bust open by the Fire. Smithfield to
Temple, Temple to Tower, molten lead swirling down
Ludgate. The Tower, you didn't have to be a teacher
to see poor Lady Jane blindfold on her knees, groping
for the block. 'Where is it? Where is it?' They wondered why so small a body gushed so much blood.

Bron walked more slowly. An early shadow lapsed.
Stuffy tourists elbowed past in paper hats. A girl's

face lay under hair built up like a golden radiator. Tall glass and steel draining the sky. Glare of news-papers...demonstration at shipyard, hymns sung for new Polaris.

This acre of London whistles at every edge. The Strict and Particular Baptist Corporation, Praise and Thanksgiving. Elliot & Niece bury you at Moderate Charges. The Old Bailey's golden floozy blind and high. Site of Newgate and cruelty, nosegays handed out to you as you left for the rope. An ancient church hanging on amongst towering offices where dull fac-es waited for loot. A Cromwell had married there. Wanted, topless choirgirls.

From *Landlord*, 1970

Henry Mayhew in a hot-air balloon

It was late in the evening (a fine autumn one) when the gun was fired that was the signal for the great gas-bag to be loosened from the ropes that held it down to the soil; and immediately the buoyant machine bounded, like a big ball, into the air...Now began that peculiar panoramic effect which is the distinguishing feature of the first portion of a view from a balloon, and which arises from the utter absence of all sense of motion in the machine itself, and the consequent transference of the movement to the ground beneath. The earth, as the aeronautic vessel glided over it, seemed positively to consist of a continuous series of scenes which were being drawn along underneath us, as if it were some diorama laid flat upon the ground, and almost gave one the notion that the world was an endless landscape stretched upon rollers, which some invisible sprites below were busy revolving for our especial amusement.

Then, as we floated along above the fields, in a line with the Thames towards Richmond, and looked over the edge of the car in which we were standing… the sight was the most exquisite visual delight ever experienced…Far beneath, in the direction we were sailing, lay the suburban fields; and here the earth, with its tiny hills and plains and streams, assumed the appearance of the little coloured plaster models of countries. The roadways striping the land were like narrow brown ribbons, and the river, which we could see winding far away, resembled a long, gray, metallic-looking snake, creeping through the fields. The bridges over the Thames were positively like planks; and the tiny black barges, as they floated along the stream, seemed no bigger than summer insects on the water. The largest meadows were about the size of green-baize table covers; and across these we could just trace the line of the South-Western Railway, with the little whiff of white steam issuing from some passing engine, and no greater in volume than the jet of vapour from an ordinary tea-kettle…

In the opposite direction to that in which the wind

was insensibly wafting the balloon, lay the leviathan Metropolis, with a dense canopy of smoke hanging over it, and reminding one of the fog of vapour that is often seen steaming up from the fields at early morning. It was impossible to tell where the monster city began or ended, for the buildings stretched not only to the horizon on either side, but far away into the distance, where, owing to the coming shades of evening and the dense fumes from the million chimneys, the town seemed to blend into the sky, so that there was no distinguishing earth from heaven...Here and there we could distinguish little bare green patches of parks, and occasionally make out the tiny circular enclosures of the principal squares, though, from the height, these appeared scarcely bigger than wafers... That little building, no bigger than one of the small china houses that are used for burning pastilles in, is Buckingham Palace—with St James's Park, dwindled to the size of a card-table, stretched out before it. Yonder is Bethlehem Hospital, with its dome, now about the same dimensions as a bell...Indeed, it was a most wonderful sight to behold that vast bricken mass of churches and hospitals, banks and prisons, palaces and workhouses, docks and refuges for the destitute, parks and squares, and courts and alleys, which make up London—all blent into one immense black spot—to look down upon the whole as the birds of the air look down upon it, and see it dwindled into a mere rubbish heap—to contemplate from afar that strange conglomeration of vice, avarice, and low cunning, of noble aspirations and humble heroism, and to grasp it in the eye, in all its incongruous integrity, at one single glance—to take, as it were, an angel's view of that huge town where, perhaps, there is more virtue and more iniquity, more wealth and more want, brought together into one dense focus than in any other part of the earth.

From *The Illustrated London News*,
18th September 1852

Joseph Conrad's Thames

After the gradual cessation of all sound and movement on the faithful river, only the ringing of ships' bells is heard, mysterious and muffled in the white vapour from London Bridge right down to the Nore, for miles and miles in a decrescendo tinkling, to where the estuary broadens out into the North Sea, and the anchored ships lie scattered thinly in the shrouded channels between the sand-banks of the Thames' mouth. Through the long and glorious tale of years of the river's strenuous service to its people these are its only breathing times.

From *The Mirror of the Sea*, 1906

G.K. Chesterton: *King's Cross Station* (1900)

This circled cosmos whereof man is god

Has suns and stars of green and gold and red,
And cloudlands of great smoke, that range o'er range
Far floating, hide its iron heavens o'erhead.

God! shall we ever honour what we are,
And see one moment ere the age expire,
The vision of man shouting and erect,
Whirled by the shrieking steeds of flood and fire?

Or must Fate act the same grey farce again,
And wait, till one, amid Time's wrecks and scars,
Speaks to a ruin here, 'What poet-race
Shot such cyclopean arches at the stars?'

Lord Byron's vision of London

A mighty mass of brick, and smoke, and shipping,
Dirty and dusky, but as wide as eye
Could reach, with here and there a sail just skipping
In sight, then lost amidst the forestry
Of masts; a wilderness of steeples peeping
On tiptoe through their sea-coal canopy;
A huge, dun cupola, like a foolscap crown
On a fool's head,—and there is London Town!

From Don Juan, Canto X, 1819–24

H.R.H. The Prince of Wales: That familiar dome

St Paul's is not just a symbol and a mausoleum for national heroes. It is also a temple which glorifies God

through the inspired expression of man's craftsman-
ship and art. Architecturally, I believe it has a character all of its own.

That familiar dome, raised high on its balustraded
drum, often appearing with a ghostly magnificence
through the London mists and river fogs. That skyline with the sentinel towers at its west end and the
chorus of spires of a hundred parish churches which
Canaletto painted in the 18th century, was without
doubt one of the architectural wonders of the world,
the equal in architecture to Shakespeare's plays.

What, then, have we done to it since the bomb-
ing? In the space of a mere fifteen years, in the '60s
and '70s, and in spite of all sorts of elaborate rules
supposedly designed to protect that great view, your
predecessors, as the planners, architects and devel-
opers of the City, wrecked the London skyline and
desecrated the dome of St Paul's.

Not only did they wreck the London skyline in
general. They also did their best to lose the great
dome in a jostling scrum of office buildings, so medi-
ocre that the only way you ever remember them is by
the frustration they induce—like a basketball team
standing shoulder-to-shoulder between you and the
Mona Lisa. In Paris, the French have built some pretty
awful tower blocks in La Défense, but can you really imagine them building those same towers around
Notre Dame? Can you imagine the Italians walling in

St Mark's in Venice or St Peter's in Rome with office blocks the size of the Pirelli building in Milan? You can't. But we've done something almost as bad, and we've done it ourselves.

And at street level, just look at Paternoster Square! Did modern planners and architects in London ever use their eyes? Those planners swept away the lanes and alleys, hidden-away squares and courtyards which in most other European countries would have been lovingly rebuilt after the War. I was in Germany a few weeks ago, and returned greatly impressed by the way in which Munich has been so carefully restored after the ravages of the War.

In devastated Warsaw, they used the paintings of Canaletto's nephew, Bellotto, as blueprints so that they could recreate the intimacy of the lost city. Lost, but found again; they brought it back from the dead. We buried the dead deeper. What did we do? Here, even the street where Shakespeare and Milton brought their manuscripts, the legendary Paternoster Row, 'The Row', the very heart of publishing since Elizabethan times, was turned into a concrete service road leading to an underground car park!

You have, ladies and gentlemen, to give this much to the Luftwaffe: when it knocked down our buildings, it didn't replace them with anything more offensive than rubble. We did that. Clausewitz called war the continuation of diplomacy by other means.

Around St Paul's, planning turned out to be the continuation of war by other means.

From a speech given at the Guildhall, 1987

D.H. Lawrence: *Parliament Hill in the Evening* (1916)

The houses fade in a melt of mist
Blotching the thick, soiled air
With reddish places that still resist
The Night's slow care.

The hopeless, wintry twilight fades,
The city corrodes out of sight
As the body corrodes when death invades
That citadel of delight.

Now verdigris smoulderings softly spread
Through the shroud of the town, as slow
Night-lights hither and thither shed
Their ghastly glow.

John Evelyn on London smog

That this glorious and ancient city, which from wood
might be rendered brick, and (like another Rome)
from brick made stone and marble; which commands
the proud ocean to the Indies, and reaches the farthest
Antipodes, should wrap her stately head in clouds of
smoke and sulphur, so full of stink and darkness, I

deplore with just indignation....The immoderate use of, and indulgence to sea-coal alone in the city of London exposes it to one of the foulest inconveniences and reproaches that can possibly befall so noble and otherwise incomparable city: and that not from the culinary fires, which for being weak and less often fed below is with such ease dispelled and scattered above as it is hardly at all discernible, but from some few particular tunnels and issues belonging only to brewers, dyers, lime-burners, salt- and soap-boilers, and some other private trades, one of whose spiracles alone does manifestly infect the air more than all the chimneys of London put together besides. And that this is not the least hyperbole, let the best of judges decide it, which I take to be our senses: whilst these are belching it forth their sooty jaws, the city of London resembles the face rather of Mount Etna, the court of Vulcan, Stromboli, or the suburbs of hell, than an assembly of rational creatures and the imperial seat of our incomparable monarch. For when in all other places the air is most serene and pure, it is here eclipsed with such a cloud of sulphur as the sun itself, which gives day to all the world besides, is hardly able to penetrate and impart it here; and the weary traveller, at many miles distance, sooner smells, than sees the city to which he repairs. This is that pernicious smoke which sullies all her glory, superinducing a sooty crust or fur upon all that it lights, spoiling the moveables, tarnishing the plate, gildings, and furniture, and corroding the very iron bars and hardest stones with those piercing and acrimonious spirits which accompany its sulphur; and executing more in one year than exposed to the pure air of the country it could effect in some hundreds.

From *Fumifugium*, 1661

William Dean Howells on London fog

Well towards fifty years had passed between my first and last visits to London, but I think I had kept for it throughout that long interval much more of the earlier sentiment than for any other city that I have known. I do not wish to be mystical, and I hesitate to say that this sentiment was continuous through the smell of the coal-smoke, or that the smoke formed a solution in which all associations were held, and from which they were, from time to time, precipitated in specific memories. The peculiar odor had at once made me at home in London, for it had probably so saturated my first consciousness in the little black, smoky town on the Ohio River, where I was born, that I found myself in a most intimate element when I now inhaled it. But apart from this personal magic, the London smoke has always seemed to me full of charm. Of course it is mostly the smoke which gives 'atmosphere', softens outlines, tenderly blurs forms, makes near and far the same, and *intenerisce il cuore*, for any him whose infant sense it bathed. No doubt it thickens the constant damp, and lends mass and viscosity to the fog; but it is over-blamed and under-praised. It is chiefly objectionable, it is wholly deplorable, indeed, when it descends in those sooty particles, the 'blacks'; but in all my London sojourns I have had but one experience of the blacks, and I will not condemn the smoke because of them. It gives a wild pathetic glamour to the late winter sunrises and the early winter sunsets, the beauty of which dwells still in my mind from my first London sojourn. In my most recent autumn, it mellowed the noons to the softest effulgence; in the summer it was a veil in the air which kept the flame of the heated term from doing its worst. It hung, diaphanous, in the dusty perspectives, but it gathered and thickened about the squares and places, and subdued all edges, so that nothing cut or hurt the vision.

From *London Films*, 1905

William Morris on pre-industrial London

Forget six counties overhung with smoke,
Forget the snorting steam and piston stroke,
Forget the spreading of the hideous town;
Think rather of the pack-horse on the down,
And dream of London, small, and white, and clean.
The air clears...

From *Earthly Paradise*, 1868–70

Karl Moritz on the prospect of London

We first descried it enveloped in a thick smoke or fog. St Paul's arose like some huge mountain above the enormous mass of smaller buildings. The Monument, a very lofty column, erected in memory of the great fire of London, exhibited to us, perhaps, chiefly on account of its immense height, apparently so disproportioned to its other dimensions (for it actually struck us as resembling rather a slender mast, towering up in immeasurable height into the clouds, than as that it really is, a stately obelisk) an unusual and singular appearance. Still we went on, and drew nearer and nearer with amazing velocity, and the surrounding objects became every moment more distinct. Westminster Abbey, the Tower, a steeple, one church, and then another, presented themselves to our view; and we could now plainly distinguish the high round chimneys on the tops of the houses, which yet seemed to us to form an innumerable number of smaller spires, or steeples.

From *Travels in England*, 1782

Oscar Wilde: *Impression du Matin* (1881)

The Thames nocturne of blue and gold
Changed to a Harmony in gray:
A barge with ochre-colored hay
Dropt from the wharf: and chill and cold

The yellow fog came creeping down
The bridges, till the houses' walls
Seemed changed to shadows, and St Paul's
Loomed like a bubble o'er the town.

Then suddenly arose the clang
Of waking life; the streets were stirred
With country waggons: and a bird
Flew to the glistening roofs and sang.

But one pale woman all alone,
The daylight kissing her wan hair,
Loitered beneath the gas lamp's flare,
With lips of flame and heart of stone.

A LITTLE LEARNING

Nowhere is the memory so highly selective as it is in the recollection of school. Byron felt moved to write affectionately of his schooldays in an eloquent tribute entitled *On a Distant View of the Village and School of Harrow on the Hill*:

> But if, through the course of the years which await me,
> Some new scene of pleasure should open to view,
> I will say, while with rapture the thought shall elate me,
> 'Oh! such were the days which my infancy knew.'

Thomas Hood, meanwhile, parodied Byron in his own, rather more prosaic, recollections in *Ode on a Distant Prospect of Clapham Academy*:

> There I was birched! there I was bred!
> There like a little Adam fed
> From Learning's woful tree!—
> The weary tasks I used to con!
> The hopeless leaves I wept upon!

The extracts in this chapter reveal some illuminating attitudes to learning and some very different approaches to the process of education. The first extract is by

William Makepeace Thackeray (1811–63), from his picaresque novel *Barry Lyndon*. The swaggering hero pours contempt on learning, the implication being that a self-made man of the world can do very well without the pretence and encumbrance of a classical education. He puts Dr Johnson and his biographer James Boswell firmly if implausibly in their places, Johnson ludicrously represented as a picture of deference, Boswell as a brash, self-righteous boor with a broad Scots accent.

In a nicely-observed vignette set in the stalls of the Drury Lane Theatre, the journalist and author Pierce Egan (1772–1849) describes a well-educated little girl reprimanding her vulgar, garrulous mother for chattering during the play. The mother roundly tells her off for getting above herself, merely on account of having had a little 'edification'. Egan is a hugely entertaining writer, an important source of information on early 19th-century London street life, manners and morals. The descriptive title of his major work says it all: *Life in London, or, The day and night scenes of Jerry Hawthorn, esq., and his elegant friend, Corinthian Tom, accompanied by Bob Logic, the Oxonian, in their rambles and sprees through the metropolis*. The second extract by Egan describes the dissolute life in public schools (well documented in the period) before the reforms of Thomas Arnold.

James Boswell in his *Life of Johnson* provides a moving vignette in which Johnson muses on the attempts of an earnest and barely educated servant to write commemorative verse. Samuel Johnson (1709–84) was an essayist, poet, lexicographer and scholar, known as 'Doctor Johnson', an enduring figure in London's literary landscape. He was a stout, bearish, ungainly man, sketched by Macaulay as 'an absent, awkward scholar, who gave strange starts and uttered strange growls, who dressed like a scarecrow and ate like a cormorant.' He is popularly remembered for his *Dictionary of the English Language* and his table talk, as reported by his lively biographers, James Boswell and Hester Thrale. He was born in Lichfield, the son of a respected but struggling bookseller. With the help of a small inheritance, his mother sent him to Oxford, but he was forced to leave after only a year, unable to afford the fees (his Doctorate was honorary, awarded much later, by Trinity College, Dublin). He married Elizabeth Porter, 'Tetty', the widow of a friend and some years older than he was. He invested much of her considerable capital, £600, in a school, Edial Hall, that failed. He set out for London accompanied by one of his pupils, David Garrick; on this Whittingtonesque trip they famously shared a horse, one walking ahead while the other rested. After slow beginnings he steadily built a reputation as a poet (*London* and *The Vanity of Human Wishes*), biographer (*Lives of the Poets*), dramatist (*Irene*, produced by David Garrick) and moral-philosophical allegorist (*The History of Rasselas, Prince of Abissinia*). At the core of his output, perhaps, are just over 200 essays he wrote over a period of two years and published in a twopenny broadsheet, *The Rambler*. These essays, the embodiment of Johnson as practical moralist, offer wisdom on an extraordinary range of topics, from the general (No. 28, 'The Various Arts of Self Delusion') to the specific (No. 207, 'The Folly of Continuing too Long upon The Stage'). Johnson kept an eccentric household in London, at any given time a shelter for friends who had fallen on hard times. Prominent in the *ménage* were his Jamaican servant Francis Barber and Hodge, his cat (*see p. 201*). Sir Joshua Reynolds, who painted Johnson several times, founded the Literary Club in Soho so as to give Johnson 'unlimited opportunities for talking'.

James Boswell (1740–95), a lawyer and diarist, was the biographer of Samuel Johnson and an entertaining source of anecdote about many other characters of the period.

The journalist and theatre manager John Hollingshead (1827–1904) describes one of the leading Ragged Schools for the poor and the challenges faced by its staff.

Museums, as much as places of entertainment, are also foundations of learning and are designed very efficiently these days to attract and instruct people who might not otherwise put Egyptian antiquities, Victorian stained glass or medieval costume high on a list of priorities. As well as the very famous collections there are some museums in London that are off the beaten track, small and easily missed. One such is Sir John Soane's Museum in Lincoln's Inn, once the home of the famous architect and collector, housing his exquisite collection of antiquities, sculpture and painting. The museum has changed little since Henry James's time and in the extract below James captures very well the way in which one's sense of time and space are subtly distorted amongst the runways, warrens, crevices and caverns of Soane's collection. A striking feature of the building is the ingenious way in which Soane lit it: pier glasses, oculi, glazed domes, niches illuminated from concealed overhead apertures all reflect and filter daylight with disarming subtlety. Henry James (1843–1916) was born in New York City and came to regard London, Venice and Paris as homes from home. In *A London Life*, the novella from which the extract below is taken, the heroine, Laura Wing, is caught in the middle of gruesome marital discord between her sister, the embittered and promiscuous Selina, and her brother-in-law, the alcoholic aristocrat Lionel Berrington. The novel exudes a disturbing aura of French naturalism and Anglo-American worldliness.

The extract from Edward Walford's *Old and New London* describes the long gone but in its day very popular collection held at Don Saltero's coffee houses in the late 17th and early 18th centuries. James Salter, known as Don Saltero, (d. c.1728) was a coffee-house proprietor of Irish origin who settled in Chelsea in about 1673. He opened his first coffee house in Lawrence St about 1695 before finally settling at 18 Cheyne Walk in 1717. His former employer Sir Hans Sloane, with whom he had travelled widely, gave him a small collection of curios, and others soon followed suit. The result was the celebrated Don Saltero's (Richard Steele gave him the mock noble nickname) with its 'ten thousand gimcracks', a popular Chelsea attraction and, in its way, the first popular 'museum'. Sadly, after Salter's death, the whole collection was put to auction and only realised just over £50, hardly a great price for an assembly of objects that included such forceful *mementi mori* as a starved cat and Mary Queen of Scots's pin-cushion.

The selection concludes with the American poet Louise Imogen Guiney (1861–1920), who likens the books in the British Museum Reading Room to a moon, reflecting light and wisdom from the sun and thus illuminating mankind's way.

Six weeks was all the schooling I ever got

So six weeks was all the schooling I ever got. And I
say this to let parents know the value of it; for though
I have met more learned book-worms in the world, especially a great hulking, clumsy, blear-eyed old doctor,
whom they called Johnson, and who lived in a court
off Fleet Street, in London, yet I pretty soon silenced
him in an argument (at 'Button's coffeehouse'); and in
that, and in poetry, and what I call natural philosophy,
or the science of life, and in riding, music, leaping,
the small-sword, the knowledge of a horse, or a main
of cocks, and the manners of an accomplished gentleman and a man of fashion, I may say for myself that
Redmond Barry has seldom found his equal. 'Sir,' said
I to Mr Johnson, on the occasion I allude to—he was
accompanied by a Mr Boswell of Scotland, and I was
presented to the club by a Mr Goldsmith, a countryman of my own—'Sir,' said I, in reply to the schoolmaster's great thundering quotation in Greek, 'you
fancy you know a great deal more than me, because
you quote your Aristotle and your Pluto; but can you
tell me which horse will win at Epsom Downs next
week?—Can you run six miles without breathing?—
Can you shoot the ace of spades ten times without
missing? If so, talk about Aristotle and Pluto to me.'

'D'ye knaw who ye're speaking to?' roared out the
Scotch gentleman, Mr Boswell, at this.

'Hold your tongue, Mr Boswell,' said the old schoolmaster. 'I had no right to brag of my Greek to the gentleman, and he has answered me very well.'

W.M. Thackeray, from *Barry Lyndon*, 1844

An episode at the Drury Lane Theatre

'Bless my heart!' said a fat lady in a back seat, 'what a noise them 'are gentlemen does make—they talk so loud there 'ant no such thing as seeing what is said—I wonder they don't make these here boxes more bigger, for I declare I'm so scrouged I'm all in a—Fanny, did you bring the rumperella for fear it should rain as we goes home?'

'Hush, Mother,' said a plump-faced little girl, who sat along side of her—'don't talk so loud, or otherwise everybody will hear you instead of the Performers, and that would be quite preposterous.'

'Don't call me *posterous*, Miss. Because you have been to school, and learnt some *edification*, you thinks you are to do as you please with me.'

Pierce Egan, from *Life in London*, 1821

Pierce Egan on the perils of public schools

The family connections and the power of purse, with which the students are aided, embolden them to assume an unbounded license, and to set at complete defiance all sober rules and regulations; and it may be justly remarked that our public seminaries are admirably situated for the indulgence of their propensities: for instance, Westminster School is fortunately situated in the immediate neighbourhood of a famous place of instruction called Tothill Fields, where every species of refined lewdness and debauchery, and manners the most depraved, are constantly exhibited; consequently they enjoy the great advantages of learning the slang language, and of hearing prime chaunts, rum glees, and kiddy catches, in the purest and most bang up style. He has likewise a fine opportunity of contracting an unalterable penchant for the frail sisterhood...cock fighting, bull and badger baiting, donkey racing, drinking, swearing, swaggering, and other refined amusements, so necessary to form the character of an accomplished gentleman.

Again, Harrow School is happily so near to the metropolis, as to afford frequent opportunities for occasional visits to similar scenes of contagion and fashionable dissipation, that the scholars do not fail to seek advantages of taking lessons in all those delectable sciences. Eton, it is true, is somewhat farther removed from the nursery of improvement, but it is near enough to Windsor, of which place it is not necessary to say much, for their Bacchanalian and Cyprian orgies, and other fashionable festivities, are well known. So...there can scarcely be a doubt of their being able to sport their figures to advantage, whenever they are let loose upon society.

From *Life in London*, 1821

When the Duke of Leeds shall married be

It is very remarkable, that [Dr Johnson] retained in his memory very slight and trivial, as well as important things. As an instance of this, it seems that an inferior domestic of the Duke of Leeds had attempted to celebrate his Grace's marriage in such homely rhymes as he could make; and this curious composition having been sung to Dr Johnson he got it by heart, and used to repeat it in a very pleasant manner. Two of the stanzas were these:—

When the Duke of Leeds shall married be
To a fine young lady of high quality,
How happy will that gentlewoman be
In his Grace of Leeds's good company.

She shall have all that's fine and fair,
And the best of silk and satin shall wear;
And ride in a coach to take the air,
And have a house in St James's Square.

To hear a man, of the weight and dignity of Johnson, repeating such humble attempts at poetry, had a very amusing effect. He, however, seriously observed of the last stanza repeated by him, that it nearly comprised all the advantages that wealth can give.

From James Boswell,
The Life of Samuel Johnson, 1791

John Hollingshead on a Ragged School

At the George Yard Ragged School, Whitechapel, conducted by the Rev. Mr Thornton, and personally superintended by Mr Holland, they have turned part of an old distillery into one of the most useful and active institutions of this kind in the metropolis, and they are already struggling with these and other difficulties. The secretary, Mr Lewis, writing January 15, 1861, says:

'We have lately had a number of boys in a most distressing state—homeless, hungry, and almost naked. The teachers and friends have done what they could to help them, and can do no more. Those who teach the "ragged band" have feeling hearts, and it is painful to lie in one's own bed and feel that there are a number of poor boys wanting even shelter these bitter nights. Should we send them away and they perish in the streets, at our doors certainly would their deaths lie. We have paid for their lodgings, at various lodging-houses, night after night; but now with this severe weather, and the mass of distress it has brought around us, matters have come to such a pass we are compelled to ask the public to lend us a helping hand in our extremity. We have taken a place to shelter them in, and earnestly ask for help to go on. Old boots and shoes, old clothes, old rugs or blankets, rice, potatoes, oatmeal, &c., will be most acceptable. To send these helpless ones adrift is, apart from anything else, to make thieves of them.'

They have gathered some four hundred children, of all ages, and of both sexes; and they give them every encouragement to consider the school as their home. They provide a meal of rice on one day, a meal of bread on another, and a meal of soup, if they can, on the third day; and they have taken eight poor castaways—nobody's children—'into the house', and are endeavouring to train them into honest working boys. The stories of destitution, cruelty, and desertion which these outcasts have to tell are more harrowing than a thousand tragedies. One has lost all traces of his parents, another is a street beggar's orphan, and another owns no parent but a drunken prostitute, who kicked him, swore at him, stabbed him in the cheek, and left a scar which he will carry to his grave. He can now find no traces of such a mother, except in the cruel mark upon his face; and is more happy, perhaps, in calling his schoolmaster father than he ever was before in his life.

The conductors of this school are anxious to fit up some kind of rough sleeping-loft for the children. They dread to let them go out into the black courts and alleys, knowing what dirt and brutality often await them. It requires very little diving behind the houses on either side of the Whitechapel main road to account for this feeling on the part of the ragged-school managers. Within a few yards of this refuge is

New Court, a nest of thieves, filled with thick-lipped, broad-featured, rough-haired, ragged women, and hulking leering men, who stand in knots, tossing for pennies, or lean against the walls at the entrances of the low courts. The houses present every conceivable aspect of filth and wretchedness; the broken windows are plastered with paper, which rises and falls when the doors of the rooms are opened: the staircases always look upon the court, as there is seldom any street door, and they are steep, winding, and covered with blocks of hard mud...The ashes lie in front of the houses; the drainage is thrown out of the windows to swell the heap; and the public privy is like a sentry-box stuck against the pump in a corner of the court. There may be as many families as there are rooms, cellars, and cupboards in a single house; forty people, perhaps, huddled together in a small dwelling; and if there is not a mixture of different families in one room it is due to the ceaseless vigilance of the sanitary officer, Inspector Price, in carrying out the Lodging-Houses Act. The lowest order of Irish, when they get an opportunity, will take a room and sub-let it to as many families as the floor will hold. Inkhorn Court is a fair sample of an Irish colony; the houses are three stories high, and there is not a corner unoccupied. Tewkesbury Buildings is a colony of Dutch Jews, and, if anything, they are a little cleaner than their Christian neighbours. George Yard is an Eng-

lish colony, numbering about a hundred families; and
Wentworth Street, Crown Court, and Castle Alley
have the same character.

From *Ragged London in 1861*

Henry James at Sir John Soane's Museum

The cab stopped at the Soane Museum, which Laura
Wing had always wanted to see, a compatriot having once told her that it was one of the most curious things in London and one of the least known.
While Mr Wendover was discharging the vehicle
she looked over the important old-fashioned square
(which led her to say to herself that London was endlessly big and one would never know all the places
that made it up) and saw a great bank of cloud hanging above it—a definite portent of a summer storm.
'We are going to have thunder; you had better keep
the cab,' she said; upon which her companion told
the man to wait, so that they should not afterwards,
in the wet, have to walk for another conveyance. The
heterogeneous objects collected by the late Sir John
Soane are arranged in a fine old dwelling-house, and
the place gives one the impression of a sort of Saturday afternoon of one's youth—a long, rummag-
ing visit, under indulgent care, to some eccentric
and rather alarming old travelled person. Our young
friends wandered from room to room and thought
everything queer and some few objects interesting;

Mr Wendover said it would be a very good place to find a thing you couldn't find anywhere else—it illustrated the prudent virtue of keeping. They took note of the sarcophagi and pagodas, the artless old maps and medals. They admired the fine Hogarths; there were uncanny, unexpected objects that Laura edged away from, that she would have preferred not to be in the room with. They had been there half an hour—it had grown much darker—when they heard a tremendous peal of thunder and became aware that the storm had broken. They watched it a while from the upper windows—a violent June shower, with quick sheets of lightning and a rainfall that danced on the pavements. They took it sociably, they lingered at the window, inhaling the odour of the fresh wet that splashed over the sultry town. They would have to wait till it had passed, and they resigned themselves serenely to this idea, repeating very often that it would pass very soon. One of the keepers told them that there were other rooms to see—that there were very interesting things in the basement. They made their way down—it grew much darker and they heard a great deal of thunder—and entered a part of the house which presented itself to Laura as a series of dim, irregular vaults—passages and little narrow avenues—encumbered with strange vague things, obscured for the time but some of which had a wicked, startling look, so that she wondered how the keepers could stay there. 'It's very fearful—it looks like a cave of idols!' she said to her companion; and then she added—'Just look there—is that a person or a thing?' As she spoke they drew nearer to the object of her reference—a figure in the middle of a small vista of curiosities, a figure which answered her question by uttering a short shriek as they approached. The immediate cause of this cry was apparently a vivid flash of lightning, which penetrated into the room and illuminated both Laura's face and that of the mysterious person. Our young lady recognised her sister, as Mrs Berrington had evidently recognised her.

From *A London Life*, 1887

Edward Walford at Don Saltero's

The following curiosities were...disposed in various parts of the coffee-room, with many others less remarkable in their names and appearance—'King James's coronation sword; King William's coronation sword and shoes; Henry VIII's coat of mail, gloves, and spurs; Queen Elizabeth's prayer-book, stirrup, and strawberry dish; the Pope's infallible candle; a set of beads, consecrated by Clement VII, made of the bones of St Anthony of Padua; a piece of the royal oak; a petrified child, or the figure of death; a curious piece of metal, found in the ruins of Troy; a pair of Saxon stockings; William the Conqueror's family sword; Oliver's broad-sword; the King of Whiddaw's

staff; Bistreanier's staff; a wooden shoe, put under
the Speaker's chair in James II's time; the Emperor
of Morocco's tobacco pipe; a curious flea-trap; an
Indian prince's crown; a starved cat, found between
the walls of Westminster Abbey when the east end
was repaired; the jaws of a wild boar that was starved
to death by his tusks growing inward; a frog, fifteen
inches long, found in the Isle of Dogs; the Stafford-
shire almanack, used when the Danes were in England; the lance of Captain TowHow-Sham, king of
the Darien Indians, with which he killed six Span-
iards, and took a tooth out of each head, and put in
his lance as a trophy of his valour; a coffin of state
for a friar's bones; a cockatrice serpent; a large snake,
seventeen feet long, taken in a pigeon-house in Su-
matra—it had in its belly fifteen fowls and five pigeons; a dolphin with a flying-fish at his mouth; a
gargulet, that Indians used to cool their water with;
a whistling arrow, which the Indians use when they
would treat of peace; a negro boy's cap, made of a
rat-skin; Mary Queen of Scots' pin-cushion; a purse
made of a spider from Antigua; manna from Canaan;
a jaw of a skate, with 500 teeth; the mermaid fish; the
wild man of the woods; the flying bull's head; and,
last of all, a snake's skin, ten feet and a half long—a
most excellent hydrometer.'

It may be added that, if we may believe Pennant,
the ex-Protector, Richard Cromwell, was one of the

regular visitors at Don Saltero's coffee-house in its earliest days. The place was one of the exhibitions which Benjamin Franklin went to see when working as a journeyman printer in London; and it is on record how that after leaving the house one day he swam from Chelsea to Blackfriars, performing sundry feats in the water as he went along.

From *Old and New London*, 1878

Louise Imogen Guiney: *In the Reading-Room of the British Museum*

Praised be the moon of books! that doth above
A world of men, the fallen Past behold,
And fill the spaces else so void and cold
To make a very heaven again thereof;
As when the sun is set behind a grove,
And faintly unto nether ether rolled,
All night his whiter image and his mould
Grows beautiful with looking on her love.

Thou therefore, moon of so divine a ray,
Lend to our steps both fortitude and light!
Feebly along a venerable way
They climb the infinite, or perish quite;
Nothing are days and deeds to such as they,
While in this liberal house thy face is bright.

THE LITERARY LIFE

Many writers are forced to work at humdrum jobs in order to support themselves and their writing. The novelist Anthony Trollope (1815–82) endured boredom, humiliation and embarrassment in the Colonel-Secretary's office of the Post Office in London. He describes with beautifully judged self-deprecation the tedious and at times morally degenerate days spent in clerical drudgery for little reward. He finally volunteered for— and got—a placement in Ireland which proved to be a financial and creative liberation. He turned many of his London experiences to good account in his novels, not least his frequent scrapes with moneylenders. The tribulations of Burgo Fitzgerald (*see p. 114*) are in part based on Trollope's own tailor's bill of £12 that grew, fed by compound interest, into a massive £200.

Other writers seek solitude. In *De Profundis* Wilde recalls his vain attempt to cloister himself in Piccadilly and work away from the domestic interruptions of his wife and children in Chelsea. He had not bargained, though, for the attentions of Lord Alfred Douglas, 'Bosie', who was broke, idle and bored and insisted on a daily programme of expensive and disruptive lunches and dinners. Wilde contrasts these bacchanals at the Café Royal or the Berkeley with the intimate—and cheap—Soho dinners he enjoyed with his lifelong friend Robert Ross. Oscar Wilde (1854–1900) was an Irish dramatist, poet, lecturer, essayist and wit, best remembered for comic plays such as *The Importance of Being Earnest* and *An Ideal Husband*; an intriguing Faustian novel, *The Picture of Dorian Gray*; and a collection of children's stories, *The Happy Prince and Other Tales*. A large, elegant, generous man of considerable charm, Wilde was much photographed, often in somewhat theatrical poses. The least affected images were taken by W. & D. Downey in May 1889 and convey something of his legendary self-assurance, geniality and sharp intellect. He gave a successful lecture tour in America (the silver miners of Leadville, whom he matched drink for drink, called him 'a bully boy with no glass eye') and for a time edited *Woman's World*. He gained some notoriety as an aesthete, Aestheticism at that time being a sketchily-defined belief in art for its own sake spiced with undertones of continental decadence. His break came in 1892 when the actor-manager George Alexander asked him to write a comedy for the St James's Theatre. The result, *Lady Windermere's Fan*, was a huge success and Wilde earned over £7000 from the first run. His famous downfall came as a result of his friendship with Lord Alfred Douglas, whose father, the Marquis of Queensberry, vehemently disapproved of Wilde. After several unpleasant confrontations, Queensberry left a card at Wilde's club bearing a misspelt but clear enough message: 'To Oscar Wilde posing as a somdomite'. Keen to see his hated father in trouble if not in prison, Douglas urged Wilde to sue for libel. Unwisely, Wilde did, with the result that Queensberry was acquitted and Wilde himself charged with homosexual offences. The consequences of his 'feasting with panthers', Wilde's memorable phrase describing the danger and excitement of entertaining male prostitutes in Piccadilly restaurants, ensured that he was found guilty and sentenced to two years' hard labour. At first this Euripidean outcome failed to shatter him; from prison he wrote forceful and eloquent letters to the *Daily Chronicle* about the terrible conditions in Reading Gaol and the inhuman treatment of child prisoners. But upon his release he spent the rest of his life in exile in Italy and France, becoming increasingly ill and dejected. Two final masterpieces were forthcoming: *The Ballad of Reading Gaol* and the long, discursive and reproachful letter to Douglas, *De Profundis*. Both are remarkable for the beautifully expressed and elevating perceptions they contain about wrongdoing and redemption.

The final extract, by the satirical poet Alexander Pope (1688–1744), is taken from his mock-epic *The Dunciad*, which laments the triumph of imbecility and lack of taste. Dulness, at her temple in the City of London, is shown enthroned, adored by talentless hacks and scribblers, while Science lies in chains, Wit is threatened with exile and Morality is tortured on the rack.

Anthony Trollope, when are you going to marry my daughter?

I do not know that I should interest my readers by saying much of my Post Office experiences in those days. I was always on the eve of being dismissed, and yet was always striving to show how good a public servant I could become, if only a chance were given me. But the chance went the wrong way. On one occasion, in the performance of my duty, I had to put a private letter containing bank-notes on the secretary's table,—which letter I had duly opened, as it was not marked private. The letter was seen by the Colonel, but had not been moved by him when he left the room. On his return it was gone. In the meantime I had returned to the room, again in the performance of some duty. When the letter was missed I was sent for, and there I found the Colonel much moved about his letter, and a certain chief clerk, who, with a long face, was making suggestions as to the probable fate of the money. 'The letter has been taken,' said the Colonel, turning to me angrily, 'and, by G——! there has been nobody in the room but you and I.' As he spoke, he thundered his fist down upon the table. 'Then,' said I, 'by G——! you have taken it.' And I also thundered my fist down;—but, accidentally, not upon the table. There was there a standing movable desk, at which, I presume, it was the Colonel's habit to write, and on this movable desk was a large bottle full of ink. My fist unfortunately came on the desk, and the ink at once flew up, covering the Colonel's face and shirt-front. Then it was a sight to see that senior clerk, as he seized a quire of blotting-paper, and rushed to the aid of his superior officer, striving to mop up the ink; and a sight also to see the Colonel, in his agony, hit right out through the blotting-paper at that senior clerk's unoffending stomach. At that moment there came in the Colonel's private secretary, with the letter and the money, and I was desired to go back to my own room. This was an incident not much in my favour, though I do not know that it did me special harm.

I was always in trouble. A young woman down in the country had taken it into her head that she would like to marry me,—and a very foolish young woman she must have been to entertain such a wish. I need not tell that part of the story more at length, other-wise than by protesting that no young man in such a position was ever much less to blame than I had been in this. The invitation had come from her, and I had lacked the pluck to give it a decided negative; but I had left the house within half an hour, going away without my dinner, and had never returned to it. Then there was a correspondence,—if that can be called a correspondence in which all the letters came from one side. At last the mother appeared at the Post Office. My hair almost stands on my head now as I remember the figure of the woman walking into the big room in which I sat with six or seven other clerks, having a large basket on her arm and an immense bonnet on her head. The messenger had vainly endeavoured to persuade her to remain in the ante-room. She followed the man in, and walking up the centre of the room, addressed me in a loud voice: 'Anthony Trollope, when are you going to marry my daughter?' We have all had our worst moments, and that was one of my worst. I lived through it, however, and did not marry the young lady. These little incidents were all against me in the office.

From Anthony Trollope's *Autobiography*, 1883

Oscar Wilde recalls the distractions imposed by Bosie

I remember, for instance, in September, '93, to select merely one instance out of many, taking a set of chambers, purely in order to work undisturbed, as I had broken my contract with John Hare, for whom I had promised to write a play, and who was pressing me on the subject. During the first week you kept away. We had, not unnaturally indeed, differed on the question of the artistic value of your translation of *Salomé*. So you contented yourself with sending me foolish letters on the subject. In that week I wrote and completed in every detail, as it was ultimately performed, the first act of an *An Ideal Husband*. The second week you returned, and my work practically had to be given up. I arrived at St James's Place every morning at 11.30 in order to have the opportunity of thinking and writing without the interruption inseparable from my own household, quiet and peaceful as that household was. But the attempt was vain. At 12 o'clock you drove up and stayed smoking cigarettes and chattering till 1.30, when I had to take you out to luncheon at the Café Royal or the Berkeley. Luncheon with its liqueurs lasted usually till 3.30. For an hour you retired to White's. At tea time you appeared again and stayed till it was time to dress for dinner. You dined with me either at the Savoy or at Tite Street [Wilde's house]. We did not separate as a rule till after midnight, as supper at Willis' had to wind up the entrancing day. That was my life for those three months, every single day, except during the four days when you went abroad. I then, of course, had to go over to Calais to fetch you back. For one of my nature and temperament it was a position at once grotesque and tragic.

You surely must realise that now. You must see now that your incapacity of being alone: your nature so exigent in its persistent claim on the attention and time of others: your lack of any power of sustained intellectual concentration: the unfortunate accident—for I like to think it was no more—that you had not been able to acquire the 'Oxford temper' in intellectual matters, never, I mean, been one who could play gracefully with ideas, but had arrived at violence of opinion merely—that all these things, combined with the fact that your desires and your interests were in Life, not in Art, were as destructive to your own progress in culture as they were to my work as an artist...Of the appalling results of my friendship with you I don't speak at present. I am thinking merely of its quality while it lasted. It was intellectually degrading to me...While you were with me you were the absolute ruin of my art, and in allowing you to stand persistently between Art and myself, I give to myself shame and blame in the fullest degree. You couldn't appreciate, you couldn't know, you couldn't understand. I had no right to expect it of you at all. Your interests were merely in your meals and moods. Your desires were simply for amusements, for ordinary or less ordinary pleasures. They were what your temperament needed, or thought it needed for the moment. I should have forbidden you my house and my chambers except when I specially invited you. I blame myself without reserve for my weakness. It was merely weakness...But in the case of an artist, weakness is nothing less than a crime when it is a weakness that paralyses the imagination.

I blame myself for having allowed you to bring me to utter and discreditable financial ruin. I remember one morning in the early October of '92, sitting in the yellowing woods at Bracknell with your mother.

At that time I knew very little of your real nature. I had stayed from a Saturday to Monday with you at Oxford. You had stayed with me at Cromer for ten days and played golf. The conversation turned on you, and your mother began to speak to me about your character. She told me of your two chief faults, your vanity, and your being, as she termed it, 'all wrong about money.' I have a distinct recollection of how I laughed. I had no idea that the first would bring me to prison and the second to bankruptcy. I thought vanity a sort of graceful flower for a young man to wear, as for extravagance—the virtues of prudence and thrift were not in my own nature or my own race. But before our friendship was one month older I began to see what your mother really meant. Your insistence on a life of reckless profusion: your incessant demands for money: your claim that all your pleasures should be paid for by me, whether I was with you or not, brought me, after some time, into serious monetary difficulties, and what made the extravagance to me, at any rate, so monotonously uninteresting, as your persistent grasp on my life grew stronger and stronger, was that the money was spent on little more than the pleasures of eating, drinking and the like. Now and then it is a joy to have one's table red with wine and roses, but you outstripped all taste and temperance. You demanded without grace and received without thanks. You grew to think that you had a sort of right to live at my expense, and in a profuse luxury to which you had never been accustomed, and which, for that reason, made your appetites all the more keen, and at the end, if you lost money gambling in some Algiers Casino, you simply telegraphed next morning to me in London to lodge the amount of your losses to your account at your bank, and gave the matter no further thought of any kind.

When I tell you that between the autumn of 1892 and the date of my imprisonment, I spent with you and on you, more than £5,000 in actual money, irrespective of the bills I incurred, you will have some idea of the sort of life on which you insisted. Do you think I exaggerate? My ordinary expenses with you for an ordinary day in London—for luncheon, dinner, supper, amusements, hansoms, and the rest of it—ranged from £12 to £20, and the week's expenses were naturally in proportion and ranged from £80 to £130. For our three months at Goring my expenses (rent, of course, included) were £1,340. Step by step with the Bankruptcy Receiver I had to go over every item of my life. It was horrible. 'Plain living and high thinking,' was, of course, an ideal you could not at that time have appreciated, but such an extravagance was a disgrace to both of us. One of the most delightful dinners I remember ever having had is one Robbie and I had together in a little Soho Café, which cost about as many shillings as my dinners to you used to cost pounds. Out of my dinner with Robbie came the first and best of all my dialogues. Idea, title, treatment, mode, everything was struck out at a 3 franc 50c. *table d'hôte*. Out of the reckless dinners with you nothing remains but the memory that too much was eaten and too much was drunk…I frankly admit that the folly of throwing away all this money on you, and letting you squander my fortune to your own hurt as well as to mine, gives to me and in my eyes a note of common profligacy to my bankruptcy that makes me doubly ashamed of it. I was made for other things.

From *De Profundis*, written 1897,
published 1905

Alexander Pope on the triumph of bad writers

Now flam'd the Dog Star's unpropitious ray,
Smote ev'ry brain, and wither'd every bay;
Sick was the sun, the owl forsook his bow'r.
The moon-struck prophet felt the madding hour:
Then rose the seed of Chaos, and of Night,
To blot out order, and extinguish light,
Of dull and venal a new world to mould,
And bring Saturnian days of lead and gold.

She mounts the throne: her head a cloud conceal'd,
In broad effulgence all below reveal'd;
('Tis thus aspiring Dulness ever shines)

Soft on her lap her laureate son reclines.

Beneath her footstool, Science groans in chains,
And Wit dreads exile, penalties, and pains.
There foam'd rebellious Logic, gagg'd and bound,
There, stripp'd, fair Rhet'ric languish'd on the ground;
His blunted arms by Sophistry are borne,
And shameless Billingsgate her robes adorn.
Morality, by her false guardians drawn,
Chicane in furs, and Casuistry in lawn,
Gasps, as they straighten at each end the cord,
And dies, when Dulness gives her page the word.

From *The Dunciad*, Book IV, 1743

HARD UP

In most cities there are two kinds of poverty. Foremost is the native kind—slum-dwellers, criminals, orphans, prostitutes—today broadly referred to as the 'under-class'. Then there is another, less readily classifiable type, suffered by species of unfortunates who started off well enough but who through fecklessness or bad luck find themselves in trouble. The term 'genteel' poverty nearly fits the bill, but it fails to describe fully the predicament of the individuals described in some of the following extracts: they come from many walks of life and might be artists, poets, heirs to fortunes, aspiring writers, dreamers, romantics. Whoever they may be, none of them seems adequately equipped for the ruthless climate of a large city and many, significantly, are outsiders who came to London to make their fortune or realise a dream.

The French poets Paul Verlaine and Arthur Rimbaud spent a tempestuous time in London between 1872 and 1874. Based in Camden, they drank and quarrelled their way round central London and the East End, often gravitating to Soho, which at that time harboured a large number of Communards, supporters of the short-lived 1871 Paris Commune formed in the aftermath of the Franco-Prussian War. Neither poet was particularly interested in politics and though they did, like Karl Marx, take advantage of the British Museum Reading Room it was more for the sake of the central heating than for political research. When the going got tough they placed advertisements, reproduced here, offering private tuition (no takers are recorded).

The painter Benjamin Robert Haydon (1786–1846), whose journals are nowadays considered rather better than his paintings, was often short of money. He describes a successful application to Thomas Coutts, the banker, for a loan.

The Victorian novelist Anthony Trollope (*see p. 53*), drawing on his own experience, is voluble on the dangers posed by London to a young man turned loose upon it with no secure way of earning a living and no fixed moral compass.

The author Julian Maclaren-Ross, the model for Anthony Powell's X Trapnel, describes the Turkish baths in Soho in the 1950s, a well-known all-night refuge for the 'genteel' homeless. Maclaren-Ross was a classic product of the literary maelstrom of Soho and Fitzrovia, two areas of London populated to this day by poets, novelists, dramatists and (these days) media creatives. In this extract he describes the still prevalent culture of scrounging money, a fine art in Soho with many dedicated practitioners. Maclaren-Ross's work is deservedly enjoying a new vogue: he was something of a dandy and Powell's character in *A Dance to the Music of Time* is a telling extrapolation of the real-life man: white corduroy suit, flamboyant cane, ever ready to spend the last shilling—his or someone else's—on a taxi.

In an eerie passage from *Athenae Oxonienses*, a biographical dictionary of Oxford University alumni by the 17th-century antiquarian Anthony à Wood, Charles I, in a secret arrangement, sends for what little remains of his once vast personal wealth.

Congenital poverty is a different thing entirely, always endemic in big cities. The novelist and biographer Geraldine Mitton is best known today for her contributions to *The Fascination of London*, a popular survey of the city organised district by district. *The Children's Book of London*, published in 1903, was a spin-off of the series and very well received. It is remarkable for the directness with which it tackles the subject of urban poverty, particularly its effect on children. Mitton's extract is followed by an evocative piece by an underrated writer, Frederick Smeeton Williams, a Congregational clergyman and railway historian who wrote about how the introduction of rail brought regeneration to some of the darker reaches of London.

James Greenwood (1832–1929) was a journalist and novelist who wrote for a number of publications including the *Pall Mall Gazette* and the *Daily Telegraph*. His account of conditions in a Whitechapel sugar bakery has great documentary value but is written with a macabre relish, a reminder that poverty on this scale could provide a lucrative source of copy for jobbing journalists—though the whiff of sensationalism that pervades Greenwood's work is often redeemed by the compelling descriptions: 'Sugar, sugar everywhere, but not a bit to eat'.

John Hollingshead (1827–1904), who in his spare time was one of Dickens's roving reporters on *Household Words*, is best remembered as the innovative manager of the Gaiety Theatre in the Strand, where he worked with Gilbert and Sullivan, Henry Irving and Offenbach (it was Hollingshead's idea to risk bringing the Can-Can, the lascivious dance from the latter's *Orpheus in the Underworld*, to the London stage). His unaffected and restrained account of life in the East End contains some memorable images.

Leçons de Français, en français...
Leçons de Français, en français—perfection,
finesses—par deux Gentlemen parisiens.
Verlaine, 8, Great College-street, Camden Town.

A French Gentleman (25), most respectably
connected, of superior education, possessing a
French diploma, thorough English, and extensive
general knowledge, wishes EMPLOYMENT as
PRIVATE SECRETARY, Travelling Companion or
Tutor. Excellent references.
Address: A.R., 25 Langham-street, W.

*Advertisements placed by Paul Verlaine
and Arthur Rimbaud, 1872–74*

The artist Benjamin Robert Haydon asks the banker Thomas Coutts for a loan
All this time I was terribly hampered for money...This
was no crime, and it was perhaps reasonable; but it
was not delicate or manly. There can be no doubt I
ought to have been helped by the State, and I should
have been if the Academy had not existed, which ob-
stinately intrigued against a vote of money either to
individuals or bodies, where Art was concerned. No
doubt there were means of earning what I wanted by
occasionally devoting myself...to portraits and small
subjects. But that always divided my mind. While a
great work was in progress I always dwelt and mused,

and eternally, as it were, kept my attention on it ; so that I began again, after an interval, as eagerly as ever. It was not so, I found, when I painted small things. I never, I must confess, tried the plan fairly, and for that I deserve censure. Be that as it may, I was resolved to go through my work, to raise loan after loan to complete it, to set my life upon a chance, and to bear the hazard of the die. But had I a right to make others share the risk ? I did not deceive them. I told the rich my condition, that I had no chance of repaying anything unless my work sold.

Fuseli told me Coutts had behaved to him about his picture of the Lazar-house in a princely way...I wrote to Mrs Coutts. An answer came from Mr Coutts peculiarly touching and characteristic, and as it is an honour to his head and his heart I insert it in full:

Strand, December, 1817

Sir,

I have considered with attention your letter, and I confess though my feelings tell me I ought not to consent to the request it contains, considering the great number of a similar kind that are at this very time before me (many of them from people who have superior claims on me for relationship and connexions of various kinds) and the impossibility of satisfying one quarter part of them, and the great doubt of any of them succeeding in any adequate manner to the ex-

pectations of the parties, or the hopes I can even imagine myself, yet I feel an inclination to put the sum
of £400 in your power, and to indulge the flattery of
seeing by that means your picture finished, and your
fortune established in the manner you have pictured,
so pleasing a matter to be accomplished, and the sum
I have advanced repaid.

On the other hand past experience almost blasts
all hopes, as I have assisted several in your line in the
course of a long life, and have never succeeded; on
the contrary I have seen their prospects disappointed,
and my money lost.

That your case may prove contrary, and that I may
see you successful, will give me great pleasure, but
indeed I must look to it with very doubtful eyes. But
the trial shall be made. All depends on your exer-
tions, and I shall say no more on the subject now, but
conclude with my good wishes.

Sir, your faithful, humble servant,
T. COUTTS

From the *Autobiography*, 1853

Trollope on the pitfalls of poverty

I came up to town, as I said before, purporting to live
a jolly life upon £90 per annum. I remained seven
years in the General Post Office, and when I left it
my income was £140. During the whole of this time

I was hopelessly in debt. There were two intervals, amounting together to nearly two years, in which I lived with my mother, and therefore lived in comfort,—but even then I was overwhelmed with debt. She paid much for me,—paid all that I asked her to pay, and all that she could find out that I owed. But who in such a condition ever tells all and makes a clean breast of it? The debts, of course, were not large, but I cannot think now how I could have lived, and sometimes have enjoyed life, with such a burden of duns as I endured…And now, looking back at it, I have to ask myself whether my youth was very wicked. I did no good in it; but was there fair ground for expecting good from me? When I reached London no mode of life was prepared for me,—no advice even given to me. I went into lodgings, and then had to dispose of my time. I belonged to no club, and knew very few friends who would receive me into their houses. In such a condition of life a young man should no doubt go home after his work, and spend the long hours of the evening in reading good books and drinking tea. A lad brought up by strict parents, and without having had even a view of gayer things, might perhaps do so. I had passed all my life at public schools, where I had seen gay things, but had never enjoyed them. Towards the good books and tea no training had been given me. There was no house in which I could habitually see a lady's face and hear

a lady's voice. No allurement to decent respectabil-
ity came in my way. It seems to me that in such circumstances the temptations of loose life will almost
certainly prevail with a young man. Of course if the
mind be strong enough, and the general stuff knitted
together of sufficiently stern material, the temptations
will not prevail. But such minds and such material
are, I think, uncommon. The temptation at any rate
prevailed with me.

I wonder how many young men fall utterly to pieces
from being turned loose into London after the same
fashion. Mine was, I think, of all phases of such life
the most dangerous. The lad who is sent to mechanical work has longer hours, during which he is kept
from danger, and has not generally been taught in
his boyhood to anticipate pleasure. He looks for hard
work and grinding circumstances. I certainly had enjoyed but little pleasure, but I had been among those
who did enjoy it and were taught to expect it. And I
had filled my mind with the ideas of such joys...

From the *Autobiography*, 1883

Julian Maclaren-Ross at the Turkish baths

I used often to lend seven and a tanner to an Irishman
known as The Toucher Malone so that he could get
himself a bed at the Turkish Baths. But I never went
to the Baths myself until last year, and then for the
same reason as The Toucher: because I had nowhere

else to sleep.

A chap called Sketchy took me there. As his nick-name implies, Sketchy made a living by sketching people in pubs and sometimes in drinking clubs. He earned enough to sleep at the Baths every night and had no possessions except the clothes he stood up in, which included a green tweed fishing hat and a coursing coat that he'd bought secondhand thirty years before and weighed nearly two stone.

When Sketchy first suggested the Baths I drew back in alarm. 'Can't afford it. Not with The Toucher there.'

'Toucher's in Dublin,' Sketchy told me. 'The entrance fee's gone up double since his day, but if you've got a quid it'll be ample. Tip the bloke on the desk and the attendant who makes your bed down a bob a-piece, and you'll have enough over for breakfast in the morning...'

The entrance to the Baths proper resembled that of a mosque, all the more so because you had to remove your shoes before going in. Even Sketchy surrendered his fishing hat and coursing coat, and we padded in our socks across a dim-lit carpeted lounge with a swimming-pool in the centre, round which ran an upper gallery decorated with a frieze of armorial bearings under a Moorish ceiling. It was one in the morning, the sound of deep breathing rose like the swish of waves from all sides, and the sight of semi-nude men reclining in deckchairs through glass doors beyond added to the sudden atmosphere of shipboard...

I was too tired to face a Turkish bath that night, and fell asleep immediately in the curtained cubicle, containing two beds, to which the attendant conducted me. Once in the night I started awake with the sound of a resounding snore ringing in my ears. This came from the dormitory on the other side of the swimming-pool and seemed to be made by a sea-lion rather than by any human agency. It died away in a shuddering sob and was succeeded by a quarter-deck voice shouting 'Steward!'

'Coming, sir!' answered a distant echo, and an awed whisper from an habitué in the bed opposite mine explained: 'It's the Admiral. Wants his tea. You'll get used to it in time, chum.' Soon a discreet tray rattled past, the Admiral grunted satisfaction, and silence settled down once more. I didn't wake again until the morning, with all the lights ablaze and the man in the next bed examining his shirt and murmuring 'Question is, will the collar do another day?' (It was a question I also might have asked my own shirt; and later, on the advice of Sketchy, I bought a nylon one which, washed in the lavabo and put to dry in the Hot room overnight, solved one problem of the nomadic existence that Bath Men are committed to.)

Breakfast—undoubtedly the best in London for half a crown: bacon, egg, chipolatas, roll and butter, pot

of tea or iced fruit-juice—was served until 9.30 a.m.
at tables in the foyer;…a momentary hush fell as the
Admiral stalked by, walrus moustache, big red shining bald head, in a suit of impeccable cut, speaking
to nobody on his way out. Then, after we'd shaved in
genuine hot water and had our shoes handed back to
us bearing a high degree of gloss (a welcome change
from most hotels, with the present shortage of staff),
we made in a body for one of the pubs nearby: open,
in this district, at eleven a.m.

I was already under the spell of this predominantly
male society, and came back night after night that
winter; I got to know the attendants by their Christian
names, was always given a cubicle well away from the
Admiral, and wandered girt with a towel through the
steam and marble slabs: even penetrating to the Very
Hot Room where the floor burnt one's foot soles and
the Africans huddled for warmth. Then my financial position suddenly changed; moreover I had to
work hard and to bid the Bath Life farewell…but one
night, up from the country, all hotels full, I pushed
the familiar door and went down the stairs expecting a big welcome below. To my surprise a strange
reception-clerk stared at me from behind the desk; a
new and taciturn attendant guided me to a bed; half
the cubicles at least were empty, and there was no
sign of Sketchy or any of the regulars. Not even the
Admiral's snores disturbed my sleep; there were no

shouts of 'Steward!' and in the morning I was given a brisk shake at 7.30.

'Sorry, sir, have to be out o' here in an hour's time—new manager's orders,' and in the next cubicle a vacuum cleaner started up. A few strangers sat without speaking at the breakfast-tables outside; others were already shaving briskly outside in the wash-room beyond; but the waiter who served me had a familiar face: he was, it turned out, the last remaining member of the old staff. 'The reg'lars? What—Sketchy and them? Lor bless you, sir, they don't come in no more. Got barred, the lot on 'em, Admiral an' all. Had an argy-bargy with the new manager, fair tartar he is, wouldn't let 'em pass the door after that. Said it was getting too much of a common lodging-house like. No, sir, I couldn't say what the trouble was all about—religious differences, somebody told me, but I wouldn't know for sure.'…

There seemed nothing to hang about for. I took out my wallet and was about to pay with a pound note when I felt a hand on my arm and turned to look into the grinning face of The Toucher Malone.

'The Night Bathers', in *Collected Memoirs*, 2004

All the wealth now in my power

'The same evening also [28th January 1649, two days before his execution], the King [Charles I] took a ring from his finger, having an emerald set therein between two

diamonds, and gave it to Mr Herbert, and commanded him, as late as 'twas, to go with it from St James's to
a lady living then in Canon Row, on the back side of
King Street, in Westminster, and to give it to her without saying anything. The night was exceeding dark,
and guards were set in several places…nevertheless,
getting the word from Col. Matth. Tomlinson, Mr
Herbert passed currently, though in all places where
sentinels were he was bid stand till the corporal had
the word from him. Being come to the lady's house, he
delivered her the ring. 'Sir,' said she, 'give me leave to
show you the way into the parlour;' where being seated, she desired him to stay till she returned. In a little
time after she came in and put into his hands a little
cabinet, closed with three seals, two of which were
the King's arms, and the third was the figure of a Roman; which done, she desired him to deliver it to the
same hand that sent the ring; which ring was left with
her; and afterwards, Mr Herbert taking his leave…he
gave the cabinet into the hands of his Majesty, who
told him that he should see it opened next morning.
Morning being come, the Bishop was early with the
King, and, after prayers, his Majesty broke the seals,
and showed them what was contained in the cabinet.
There were diamonds and jewels—most part broken
Georges and Garters. 'You see,' said he, 'all the wealth
now in my power to give to my children.'

From *Athenae Oxonienses*, 1691–92

Geraldine Edith Mitton on poor London children

In the streets where these children live everything is
dirty and nasty. A number of families live together
in one house, perhaps even in one room, for I have
heard of rooms where each family had a corner. The
women never do anything more than they can help.
They never mend their old dresses, or wash themselves or their children, or try to cook nicely; they
do nothing. They spend the day sitting on their dirty
doorsteps, with the youngest baby on their knees,
and their hair is all uncombed, and their dresses are
filthy and torn, and they shout out to other women
across the street, and make remarks on anyone who
happens to pass. The poor little baby gets dreadful
things to eat—things that you would think would kill
an ordinary child—bits of herring or apple, and anything else its mother eats, and sometimes even sips of
beer or gin. If it cries, it is joggled about or slapped,
and as soon as ever it is able to sit up, it is put down
on the pavement among a number of other dirty, un-
tidy children and left to take care of itself. When a
little girl is seven she is thought quite old enough to
look after all the younger ones, and on Saturdays she
goes off with other little girls, pushing a rickety old
perambulator or a wooden cart, with perhaps two babies in it and several smaller children hanging on to
her skirt; and she goes down the foul street and on
until she comes to a tiny little bit of ground, where

there are seats and some bushes and hard paths, and this is a playground. But what do you think it really has been? A graveyard, and there are still graves and big stones, showing that people have been buried there long years ago. But the children who play in it do not mind this at all; they sit on the graves, and think that they are very lucky to get this place away from the street…

Well, of course, there are many other sorts of children in London besides these…Many, very many, of the children have no playground at all but the street, the pavement, where people are passing all the time. They sit on the doorsteps and breathe in the dust, and all their playthings, if they have any—and even their food—are often thick with dust. I have seen a child rubbing a bit of bread-and-jam up and down on the dirty stone before it eats it. But the rich children and the poor children do not often meet, for if the rich children go through the streets in the poorer parts they are in motor-cars or cabs, and in their part of the park there are not many poor children, while in the parks where the poor children go you do not find many rich ones…And many rich children grumble all the time if they do not have everything they want, and never think of their poor little brothers and sisters, who would snatch eagerly at many of the things they throw away.

Have you heard the story of the Pied Piper of

Hamelin, who piped so wonderfully that he could make anything follow him when he liked, and how he piped so that all the rats ran after him, and he led them to the river and they were drowned? When he asked the mayor and chief men in the town to be paid for what he had done, they laughed, and said: 'No, now the rats are dead, you can't make them alive again; we have got what we wanted, and we won't pay you.' So the piper was very angry, and piped another tune, and all the children in the town followed him; and he led them on and on toward a great mountain, where a cave opened suddenly, and they all went in, and were never seen again. I think if that Pied Piper came to London he would find very many more different sorts of children than ever he found in Hamelin, where—

> 'Out came the children running:
> All the little boys and girls,
> With rosy checks and flaxen curls,
> And sparkling eyes, and teeth like pearls,
> Tripping and skipping ran merrily after
> The wonderful music with shouting and laughter.'

There would be London children whose eyes did not sparkle, and who had almost forgotten to laugh, as well as those like the children of Hamelin, who were so bright and so gay.

From *The Children's Book of London*, 1903

F.S. Williams on the coming of the railway

Old St Pancras churchyard was invaded, and Agar
Town almost demolished. Yet those who knew this
district at that time have no regret at the change. Time
was when the wealthy owner of a large estate had
lived here in his mansion; but after his departure the
place became a very 'abomination of desolation'. In
its centre was what was termed La Belle Isle, a dreary
and unsavoury locality, abandoned to mountains of
refuse from the metropolitan dust-bins, strewn with
decaying vegetables and foul-smelling fragments of
what once had been fish, or occupied by knackers'-
yards and manure-making, bone-boiling, and soap-
manufacturing works, and smoke-belching potteries
and brick-kilns. At the broken doors of mutilated
houses canaries still sang, and dogs lay basking in the
sun, as if to remind one of the vast colonies of bird-
fanciers and dog-fanciers who formerly made Agar
Town their abode; and from these dwellings came
out wretched creatures in rags and dirt, and searched
amid the far-extending refuse for the filthy treasure
by the aid of which they eked out a miserable liveli-
hood; whilst over the whole neighbourhood the gas-
works poured forth their mephitic vapours, and the
canal gave forth its rheumatic dampness, extracting
in return some of the more poisonous ingredients in
the atmosphere, and spreading them upon the surface of the water in a thick scum of various and omi-

nous hues. Such was Agar Town before the Midland
Railway came into the midst of it.

> From *The Midland Railway: its Rise and Progress*
> *a Narrative of Modern Enterprise*, 1876

James Greenwood in a sugar factory

It was a sort of handy outer warehouse, that to which
we were first introduced—a low-roofed, dismal place
with grated windows, and here and there a foggy little
gas-jet burning blear-eyed against the wall. The walls
were black—not painted black. As far as one might
judge they were bare brick, but 'basted' unceasingly
by the luscious steam that enveloped the place, they
had become coated with a thick preserve of sugar
and grime. The floor was black, and all corrugated
and hard, like a public thoroughfare after a shower
and then a frost. The roof was black, and pendent
from the great supporting posts and balks of timber
were sooty, glistening icicles and exudings like those
of the gum-tree. 'Sugar, sugar everywhere, but not a
bit to eat.' Exactly the Bogeydom to which should be
consigned for a term, according to the degree of their
iniquity, the owners of larcenous little fingers so persistent in their attacks on the domestic sugar-basin.
At the extremity of this gloomy cave, and glowing
duskily at the mouth of a narrow passage, was dimly
visible a gigantic globular structure in bright copper,
and hovering about it a creature with bare arms and

chest all grizzly-haired, with a long bright rod of iron in his grasp, which incessantly he waved about the mighty cauldron; this was doubtless the Sugar Ogre himself, in waiting for juvenile delinquents.

Being in no dread of the ogre, however, we approached him, and discovered him to be a very civil fellow, quietly minding his business. The copper structure above-mentioned proved to be nothing more necromantic than a gigantic pan, in which were, gently seething, ten tons of liquid sugar…In the side of it there was a small disc of glass, and looking through it one could get a glimpse of the bubbling straw-coloured mass within. The iron rod the guardian of the pan called a 'key', if I rightly remember, and his sole occupation appeared to consist in dipping it in at a little hole in the vessel's side, and withdrawing it again, along with a little blob of melted sugar, which he took between his finger and thumb, and drew out and examined by the light of the gas.

From this we were conducted to the factory where the manufacturers of moist sugar were working. It… was not a nice-looking place that to which we were introduced…The place was nothing but a vast cellar underground, and lit from without only by a window here and there high up where the street pavement was, and as closely grated as though it were an object to keep flies out of the factory. The heat was sickening and oppressive, and an unctuous steam, thick and foggy, filled the cellar from end to end. Presently, however, when one's eyes grew somewhat accustomed to the gloom, a spectacle of a novel and startling character was presented. Seeming, as it were, to grow out of the dense haze, busy figures appeared. Black and white figures running about, and flitting and skipping in the most extraordinary manner. Watching the figures, however, they were presently discovered to be men in a condition of at least semi-nudity. On one side of the cellar were two gigantic pans of sugar, melted and hot and smoking, and out of these the labourers, naked but for a covering for their legs and some sort of apron, and their bodies bathed in sweat, and their fair hair reeking and hanging lank about their wan faces, scooped up the liquor into the pails, that would contain half a hundred weight, and hurried across the cellar to deposit it in vast revolving basins set in motion at lightning speed by machinery, and where the brown sugar was bleached and dried, to be presently shovelled out and added to the great heap that reached high nearly as the ceiling. Regarding the close, reeking, stifling place, the disgusting atmosphere, the incessant toil (machinery will not wait), and the disgusting conditions of it, the validity of the Irish labourer's objection became manifest; better a hod of bricks with a sixty-round ladder to mount out in the open air than such mean, enervating drudgery as this. 'They'd be dead without their beer unlimited,' remarked our guide. 'And does it not hurt them ?' 'Well, it helps to knock them off, I dare say.' So that it amounts to the same thing, only that the unlimited beer-drinker of the sugar bakery has the advantage of lengthy dying...

'I should imagine that you were not much addicted to the consumption of sugar,' I remarked to our guide.

'I can never taste it; it has no taste, no more has nothing for me,' he answered; and one could easily understand how that happened.

From *The Wilds of London*, 1876

John Hollingshead on a rude love of flowers

In one court I saw a singular blind labourer, who was out of work in consequence of the frost. He got his living by reading the Bible in the street, feeling the raised letters with his hand, and he complained that he could do nothing now because 'the touch was cold.' He staggered over the mud heaps with a thin stick, and disappeared in the dark, cellar-like lower room of a ragged-school refuge for outcasts. In some of these repulsive courts the inhabitants cling to a rude love of flowers, and many an unsightly window-ledge is fitted up to resemble a garden enclosure, with miniature railings and gates.

From *Ragged London in 1861*

AT HOME

The domestic sphere also has its place in London literature. Jane Austen (1775–1817) sets part of *Sense and Sensibility* in the capital, and the extract quoted here shows the sisters Elinor and Marianne recently arrived in town. Marianne's only interest is in her faithless lover Willoughby; her faithful suitor Colonel Brandon is ignored, and the tactless Mrs Jennings (in whose house the girls are staying) does not help matters.

Tea, by the Edwardian short-story writer Saki (*see p. 167*), begins with its hero setting out to propose marriage to the eminently suitable Miss Sebastable. Meditations on the irritating gentility of the afternoon tea table, over which the lovely Joan will preside with awful inevitability, day after day, cause him to change his mind—utterly unprepared for the consequences.

The painter Benjamin Robert Haydon (*see p. 66*) entertains Wordsworth and Keats at a tipsy dinner party held in his studio. The episode is chiefly notable for the presence of an interloper, a dull yet insistent civil servant who persists in asking Wordsworth, never the most forthcoming of conversationalists, a series of asinine questions. Keats, judiciously curled up in the corner with a book, is on the verge of hysterics as Charles Lamb becomes steadily drunker. In another extract from Haydon, just after he had applied to Coutts for a loan, (*see p. 69*), we meet Coutts's wife, the former actress Harriet Mellon. Coutts's marriage (he was 79 and she 37) enraged his three daughters who feared that Harriet would inherit the lion's share of their father's money. She did, and though each of the Coutts girls had married very well, they never recovered from the actress's triumph. After Coutts's death, Harriet plunged gaily on and further up the social scale, marrying the 9th Duke of St Albans in 1827: she by now was 49, he 26. Her final flourish was elegantly appropriate. When she died she left all her money to her favourite amongst Thomas Coutts's grandchildren, Angela. Angela subsequently became famous as Baroness Burdett-Coutts, one of the great women philanthropists of the 19th century (though in her private life she proved rather closer in temperament to her lively step-grandmother. To the great consternation of her family and friends, Angela married her American secretary, William Ashmead Bartlett: she was 67, he 26). The extract quoted below shows how differently she is expected to behave as Mrs Coutts from what she had been as Miss Mellon.

Two poems inspired by famous houses follow. In the first, by Thomas Hardy, the poet speculates that while Keats's remains are buried in Rome, his spirit is perpetually drawn back to the Hampstead garden where he wrote the *Ode to a Nightingale*. Tennyson laments his friend Arthur Henry Hallam, a promising poet who died tragically young and who lived for a time in Wimpole St.

Other kinds of home also appear in this chapter. The loneliness of bedsit land is well known to this day. Thomas Burke (1886–1945) describes a bleak interlude in Kingsland Road, Hackney, when, as a penniless aspiring author, he is given notice by his landlady. He is saved from the 'morchery' by a kindly fellow lodger.

The final extract is about the Foundling Hospital in Bloomsbury, which during the course of its existence (1739–1954) was home to many thousands of abandoned children. The author is the journalist, magazine editor and genealogist Edward Walford (1823–97).

Jane Austen on two young ladies at home

Marianne's [letter] was finished in a very few minutes; in length it could be no more than a note; it
was then folded up, sealed, and directed with eager
rapidity. Elinor thought she could distinguish a large
W in the direction; and no sooner was it complete
than Marianne, ringing the bell, requested the footman who answered it to get that letter conveyed for
her to the two-penny post. This decided the matter at
once. Her spirits still continued very high; but there
was a flutter in them which prevented their giving
much pleasure to her sister, and this agitation increased as the evening drew on. She could scarcely
eat any dinner, and when they afterwards returned
to the drawing room, seemed anxiously listening to
the sound of every carriage. It was a great satisfaction
to Elinor that Mrs Jennings, by being much engaged
in her own room, could see little of what was passing. The tea things were brought in, and already had
Marianne been disappointed more than once by a rap
at a neighbouring door, when a loud one was suddenly heard which could not be mistaken for one at
any other house. Elinor felt secure of its announcing
Willoughby's approach, and Marianne, starting up,
moved towards the door. Everything was silent; this
could not be borne many seconds; she opened the
door, advanced a few steps towards the stairs, and
after listening half a minute, returned into the room

in all the agitation which a conviction of having heard him would naturally produce; in the ecstasy of her feelings at that instant she could not help exclaiming, 'Oh, Elinor, it is Willoughby, indeed it is!' and seemed almost ready to throw herself into his arms, when Colonel Brandon appeared. It was too great a shock to be borne with calmness, and she immediately left the room. Elinor was disappointed too; but at the same time her regard for Colonel Brandon ensured his welcome with her; and she felt particularly hurt that a man so partial to her sister should perceive that she experienced nothing but grief and disappointment in seeing him. She instantly saw that it was not unnoticed by him, that he even observed Marianne as she quitted the room, with such astonishment and concern, as hardly left him the recollection of what civility demanded towards herself.

'Is your sister ill?' said he.

Elinor answered in some distress that she was, and then talked of head-aches, low spirits, and over fatigues; and of every thing to which she could decently attribute her sister's behaviour.

He heard her with the most earnest attention, but seeming to recollect himself, said no more on the subject, and began directly to speak of his pleasure at seeing them in London, making the usual inquiries about their journey, and the friends they had left behind. In this calm kind of way, with very little interest on either side, they continued to talk, both of them out of spirits, and the thoughts of both engaged elsewhere. Elinor wished very much to ask whether Willoughby were then in town, but she was afraid of giving him pain by any enquiry after his rival; and at length, by way of saying something, she asked if he had been in London ever since she had seen him last.

'Yes,' he replied, with some embarrassment, 'almost ever since; I have been once or twice at Delaford for a few days, but it has never been in my power to return to Barton.'

This, and the manner in which it was said, immediately brought back to her remembrance all the circumstances of his quitting that place, with the uneasiness and suspicions they had caused to Mrs Jennings, and she was fearful that her question had implied much more curiosity on the subject than she had ever felt.

Mrs Jennings soon came in. 'Oh! Colonel,' said she, with her usual noisy cheerfulness, 'I am monstrous glad to see you—sorry I could not come before—beg your pardon, but I have been forced to look about me a little, and settle my matters; for it is a long while since I have been at home, and you know one has always a world of little odd things to do after one has been away for any time; and then I have had Cartwright to settle with—Lord, I have been as busy as a bee ever since dinner! But pray, Colonel, how came you to conjure out that I should be in town today?'

'I had the pleasure of hearing it at Mr Palmer's, where I have been dining.'

'Oh, you did; well, and how do they all do at their house? How does Charlotte do? I warrant you she is a fine size by this time.'

'Mrs Palmer appeared quite well, and I am commissioned to tell you, that you will certainly see her to-morrow.'

'Ay, to be sure, I thought as much. Well, Colonel, I have brought two young ladies with me, you see—that is, you see but one of them now, but there is another somewhere. Your friend, Miss Marianne, too—which you will not be sorry to hear. I do not know what you and Mr Willoughby will do between you about her. Ay, it is a fine thing to be young and handsome. Well! I was young once, but I never was very handsome—worse luck for me. However, I got a very good husband, and I don't know what the greatest beauty can do more. Ah! poor man! he has been dead these eight years and better. But Colonel, where have you been to since we parted? And how does your business go on? Come, come, let's have no secrets among friends.'

He replied with his accustomary mildness to all her inquiries, but without satisfying her in any. Elinor now began to make the tea, and Marianne was obliged to appear again. After her entrance, Colonel Brandon became more thoughtful and silent than he had been before, and Mrs Jennings could not prevail on him to stay long. No other visitor appeared that evening, and the ladies were unanimous in agreeing to go early to bed.

From *Sense and Sensibility*, 1811

Saki on a young man's dread of the teapot

[James Cushat-Prinkly's] musings were interrupted by the sound of a clock striking the half-hour. Half-past four. A frown of dissatisfaction settled on his face. He would arrive at the Sebastable mansion just at the hour of afternoon tea. Joan [to whom he plans to propose] would be seated at a low table, spread with an array of silver kettles and cream-jugs and delicate porcelain tea-cups, behind which her voice would tinkle pleasantly in a series of little friendly questions about weak or strong tea, how much, if any, sugar, milk, cream, and so forth. 'Is it one lump? I forgot. You do take milk, don't you? Would you like some more hot water, if it's too strong?'

Cushat-Prinkly had read of such things in scores of novels, and hundreds of actual experiences had told him that they were true to life. Thousands of women, at this solemn afternoon hour, were sitting behind dainty porcelain and silver fittings, with their voices tinkling pleasantly in a cascade of solicitous little questions. Cushat-Prinkly detested the whole system of afternoon tea. According to his theory of life a woman should lie on a divan or couch, talking with incomparable charm or looking unutterable thoughts, or merely silent as a thing to be looked on, and from behind a silken curtain a small Nubian page should silently bring in a tray with cups and dainties, to be accepted silently, as a matter of course, without drawn-out chatter about cream and sugar and hot water. If one's soul was really enslaved at one's mistress's feet how could one talk coherently about weakened tea? Cushat-Prinkly had never expounded his views on the subject to his mother; all her life she had been accustomed to tinkle pleasantly at tea-time behind dainty porcelain and silver, and if he had spoken to her about divans and Nubian pages she would have urged him to take a week's holiday at the seaside. Now, as he passed through a tangle of small streets that led indirectly to the elegant Mayfair terrace for which he was bound, a horror at the idea of confronting Joan Sebastable at her tea-table seized on him. A momentary deliverance presented itself; on one floor of a narrow little house at the noisier end of Esquimault Street lived Rhoda Ellam, a sort of remote cousin, who made a living by creating hats out of costly materials. The hats really looked as if they had come from Paris; the cheques she got for them unfortunately never looked as if they were going to Paris. However, Rhoda appeared to find life amusing and to have a fairly good time in spite of her straitened circumstances. Cushat-Prinkly decided to climb up to her floor and defer by half-an-hour or so the important business which lay before him; by spinning out his visit he could contrive to reach the Sebastable mansion after the last vestiges of dainty porcelain had been cleared away.

Rhoda welcomed him into a room that seemed to do duty as workshop, sitting-room, and kitchen combined, and to be wonderfully clean and comfortable at the same time.

'I'm having a picnic meal,' she announced. 'There's caviare in that jar at your elbow. Begin on that brown bread-and-butter while I cut some more. Find yourself a cup; the teapot is behind you. Now tell me about hundreds of things.'

She made no other allusion to food, but talked amusingly and made her visitor talk amusingly too. At the same time she cut the bread-and-butter with a masterly skill and produced red pepper and sliced lemon, where so many women would merely have produced reasons and regrets for not having any...

'And now tell me why you have come to see me,' said Rhoda suddenly...

Some forty minutes later James Cushat-Prinkly returned to the bosom of his family, bearing an important piece of news.

'I'm engaged to be married,' he announced.

A rapturous outbreak of congratulation and self-applause broke out.

'Ah, we knew! We saw it coming! We foretold it weeks ago!'

'I'll bet you didn't,' said Cushat-Prinkly. 'If any one had told me at lunch-time to-day that I was going to ask Rhoda Ellam to marry me and that she was going to accept me I would have laughed at the idea.'...

On a September afternoon of the same year, after the honeymoon in Minorca had ended, Cushat-Prinkly came into the drawing-room of his new house in Granchester Square. Rhoda was seated at a low table, behind a service of dainty porcelain and gleaming silver. There was a pleasant tinkling note in her voice as she handed him a cup.

'You like it weaker than that, don't you? Shall I put some more hot water to it? No?'

From *Tea*, 1919

Benjamin Robert Haydon's 'Immortal Evening'

In the morning of this delightful day [28th Dec], a gentleman, a perfect stranger, had called on me. He said he knew my friends, had an enthusiasm for Wordsworth and begged I would procure him the happiness of an introduction. He told me he was a comptroller of stamps, and often had correspondence with the poet. I thought it a liberty; but still, as he seemed a gentleman, I told him he might come.

When we retired to tea we found the comptroller.

In introducing him to Wordsworth I forgot to say
who he was. After a little time the comptroller looked
down, looked up and said to Wordsworth, 'Don't you
think, sir, Milton was a great genius?' Keats looked
at me, Wordsworth looked at the comptroller. Lamb
who was dozing by the fire turned round and said,
'Pray, sir, did you say Milton was a great genius?' 'No,
sir; I asked Mr Wordsworth if he were not.' 'Oh,' said
Lamb, 'then you are a silly fellow.' 'Charles! my dear
Charles!' said Wordsworth; but Lamb, perfectly innocent of the confusion he had created, was off again
by the fire.

After an awful pause the comptroller said, 'Don't
you think Newton a great genius?' I could not stand it
any longer. Keats put his head into my books. Ritchie squeezed in a laugh. Wordsworth seemed asking
himself, 'Who is this?' Lamb got up, and taking a
candle, said, 'Sir, will you allow me to look at your
phrenological development?' He then turned his back
on the poor man, and at every question of the comptroller he chaunted,

'Diddle diddle dumpling, my son John
Went to bed with his breeches on.'

The man in office, finding Wordsworth did not
know who he was, said in a spasmodic and half-
chuckling anticipation of assured victory, 'I have had
the honour of some correspondence with you, Mr
Wordsworth.' 'With me, sir?' said Wordsworth, 'not

that I remember.' 'Don't you, sir? I am a comptroller of stamps.' There was a dead silence; the comptroller evidently thinking that was enough. While we were waiting for Wordsworth's reply, Lamb sung out

'Hey diddle diddle,

The cat and the fiddle.'

'My dear Charles!' said Wordsworth, 'Diddle diddle dumpling, my son John,' chaunted Lamb, and then rising, exclaimed, 'Do let me have another look at that gentleman's organs.'

Keats and I hurried Lamb into the painting-room, shut the door and gave way to inextinguishable laughter. Monkhouse followed and tried to get Lamb away. We went back but the comptroller was irreconcilable. We soothed and smiled and asked him to supper. He stayed though his dignity was sorely affected. However, being a good-natured man, we parted all in good-humour, and no ill effects followed.

All the while, until Monkhouse succeeded, we could hear Lamb struggling in the painting-room and calling at intervals, 'Who is that fellow? Allow me to see his organs once more.'

It was indeed an immortal evening. Wordsworth's fine intonation as he quoted Milton and Virgil, Keats' eager inspired look, Lamb's quaint sparkle of lambent humour, so speeded the stream of conversation, that in my life I never passed a more delightful time. All our fun was within bounds. Not a word passed that an apostle might not have listened to. It was a night worthy of the Elizabethan age, and my solemn *Jerusalem* flashing up by the flame of the fire, with Christ hanging over us like a vision, all made up a picture which will long glow upon 'that inward eye which is the bliss of solitude'.

Keats made Ritchie promise he would carry his *Endymion* to the great desert of Sahara and fling it in the midst.

Poor Ritchie went to Africa, and died, as Lamb foresaw, in 1819. Keats died in 1821, at Rome. C. Lamb is gone, joking to the last. Monkhouse is dead, and Wordsworth and I are the only two now living of that glorious party.

From the *Autobiography*, 1853

Benjamin Robert Haydon on the metamorphosis of Harriet Mellon

I had known Mrs Coutts when Miss Mellon, and dined with her with Maria Foote at Holly House, where she was living then under the protection of Mr Coutts, but certainly not in vice. It was a curious scene! so exactly what is described in *Gil Blas*. The rich banker and the gay actress, splendour and vulgarity, charity and extravagance, fun and frolic. There was a room at Holly House called the 'fun-room', without chair or table. It was for dancing and romping: here we all played at blind man's buff. It is my honest conviction there was nothing in Harriet Mellon but a girlish, romping, full-hearted, rich enjoyment at seeing every man, woman and child about her as happy as herself.

She was thoughtless in caring nothing about appearances.

After this kindest of all kind letters [see p. 69], and after her marriage to Mr Coutts, a day was appointed for me to call in Piccadilly. I did call, and after a reasonable time Mr Coutts came in leaning on her arm.

A look from her at once told me all was altered. No more 'fun-rooms'. I bowed with stately gravity, and he welcomed me and shook my hand. We then walked into the dining-room where he had got a very fine copy from Guido's *Aurora* in the Rospigliosi palace. All went on with gravity and decorum till we came to a bust of Mr Coutts by Nollekens. Nolly was a character. Harriet Mellon's love of humour made her forget Mrs Coutts' sense of dignity. She went off like a rocket and mimicked Nolly's manner to perfection. But times were altered; she was the great banker's wife, I his suppliant for cash; freedoms must be over. Mr Coutts gave her a look which iced her. In a minute or two she curtsied low to me, and swept out of the room; but she could not help turning that eye of hers as she went. A glance was enough to convince me she was Harriet Mellon still.

Mr Coutts now began, solemn and kind; he had placed the money to my account. I gave him my note-

of-hand, and shortly took my leave with unaffected
gratitude.

From the *Autobiography*, 1853

Thomas Hardy: *At a House in Hampstead* (1920)

O poet, come you haunting here
Where streets have stolen up all around,
And never a nightingale pours one
 Full-throated sound?

Drawn from your drowse by the Seven famed Hills,
Thought you to find all just the same
Here shining, as in hours of old,
 If you but came?

What will you do in your surprise
At seeing that changes wrought in Rome
Are wrought yet more on the misty slope
 One time your home?

Will you wake wind-wafts on these stairs?
Swing the doors open noisily?
Show as an umbraged ghost beside
 Your ancient tree?

Or will you, softening, the while
You further and yet further look,
Learn that a laggard few would fain
 Preserve your nook?

—Where the Piazza steps incline,
And catch late light at eventide,
I once stood, in that Rome, and thought,
　　'Twas here he died.'

I drew to a violet-sprinkled spot,
Where day and night a pyramid keeps
Uplifted its white hand, and said,
　　'Tis there he sleeps.'

Pleasanter now it is to hold
That here, where sang he, more of him
Remains than where he, tuneless, cold,
　　Passed to the dim.

Alfred, Lord Tennyson at no. 67 Wimpole Street

Dark house, by which once more I stand
Here in the long unlovely street,
Doors, where my heart was used to beat
So quickly, waiting for a hand,—
A hand that can be clasped no more,—
Behold me, for I cannot sleep,
And like a guilty thing I creep
At earliest morning to the door.
He is not here; but far away
The noise of life begins again,
And ghastly through the drizzling rain
On the bald street breaks the blank day.

From *In Memoriam*, 1849

Thomas Burke on loneliness in Hackney

I remember, finally, sloughing through Bishopsgate into Norton Folgate, when I was down to fifteen-and-sixpence. In Norton Folgate I found a timid co-coa-room, and, careless of the future, I entered and gorged. Sausages...mashed...bread...tomatoes...pints of hot tea.... Too, I found sage wisdom in the counter-boy. He had been through it. We put the matter into committee, and it was discussed from every possible point of view. I learnt that I could get a room for next to nothing round about there, and that there was nothing like studying the 'Sits. Vacant' in the papers at the Library; or, if there was anything like it, it was trusting to your luck. No sense in getting the bleed-ing pip. As he was eighteen and I was seventeen, I took his counsel to heart, and, fired with a repletion of sausage and potato, I stalked lodgings through the forests of Kingsland Road and Cambridge Road. In the greasy, strewn highway, where once the Auton-omie Club had its home, I struck Cudgett Street—a narrow, pale cul-de-sac, containing fifty dilapidated cottages; and in the window of the first a soiled card: 'One Room to Let'.

The doorstep, flush with the pavement, was crum-bling. The door had narrowly escaped annihilation by fire; but the curtains in the front-room window were nearly white. Two bare-armed ladies, with skirts hiked up most indelicately behind them, were sloshing down their respective doorsteps, and each wall was ragged with five or six frayed heads thrust from upper windows for the silken dalliance of conversation. However, it was sanctuary. It looked cheap. I knocked.

A lady in frayed alpaca, carrying a house-flannel, came to hearken. 'Oh, yerss. Come in. Half a jiff till I finished this bottom stair. Now then—whoa!—don't touch that banister; it's a bit loose. Ver narsely furnished you'll find it is. There. Half-a-crown a week. Dirt cheap, too. Why, Mrs Over-the-Road charges four for hers. But I can't. I ain't got the cheek.'

I tripped over the cocoanut mat. The dulled windows were draped with a strip of gauze. The 'narse furnicher' wasn't there. There was a chest of drawers whose previous owner had apparently been in the habit of tumbling into bed by candle-light and leaving it to splutter its decline and shed its pale blood where it would. The ceiling was picked out with flyspots. It smelt—how shall I give it to you? The outgoing tenant had obviously used the hearth as a spittoon. He had obviously supped nightly on stout and fish-and-chips. He had obviously smoked the local Cavendish. He had obviously had an acute objection to draughts of any kind. The landlady had obviously 'done up' the room once a week.... Now perhaps you get that odour.

But the lady at my side, seeing hesitation, began a

kind of pæan on the room. She sang it in its complete beauty. She dissected it, and made a panegyric on the furniture in comparison with that of Mrs Over-the-Road. She struck the lyre and awoke a louder and loftier strain on the splendour of its proportions and symmetry—'heaps of room here to swing a cat'—and her rapture and inspiration swelled as she turned herself to the smattering price charged for it. On this theme she chanted long and lovingly and a hundred coloured, senescent imageries leaped from the song.

Of course, I had to take it. And towards late afternoon, when the grey cloak of twilight was beginning to be torn by the gas lamps, I had pulled the whole place to pieces and found out what made it work. I had stood it on its head. I had reversed it, and armlocked it, and committed all manner of assaults on it. I had found twenty old cigarette ends under the carpet, and entomological wonders in the woodwork of the window. Fired by my example, the good lady came up to help, and when I returned from a stroll she had garnished it. Two chairs, on which in my innocence I sat, were draped with antimacassars. Some portraits of drab people, stiffly posing, had been placed on the mantelshelf, and some dusty wool mats, set off with wax flowers, were lighting the chest of drawers to sudden beauty. In my then mood the false luxury touched me curiously.

There I was and there I stayed in slow, mortifying idleness. *You* get stranded in Kingsland Road for a fortnight...I wish you would. It would teach you so many things. For it is a district of cold, muddy squalor that it is ashamed to own itself...I was miserably, unutterably lonely. I developed a temper of acid. I looked on the world, and saw all things bitter and wicked. The passing of a rich carriage exasperated me to fury: I understood in those moments the spirit that impels men to throw bombs at millionaires and royalties. Among the furious wilds of Kingsland, Hackney, and Homerton I spent my rage. There seemed to be no escape, no outlet, no future. Sometimes I sat in that forlorn little room; sometimes I went to bed; sometimes I wandered and made queer acquaintance at street corners; sometimes I even scanned that tragic column of the *Daily Telegraph* Situations Vacant. Money went dribbling away. At 'Dirty Dick's' you can get a quartern of port for threepence, and gin is practically given away. Drink is a curse, I know, but there are innumerable times when it has saved a man from going under...I wish temperance fiends would recognise this...

Next day, I had no food at all, and in the evening I sprawled on the bed. Then things happened.

The opposite room on the same landing had been let to a girl who worked, so I understood from my hostess, at the cork factory close at hand. She came home every evening at about six, and the little wretch invariably had a hot meal with her tea. It was carried up from below. It was carried past my door. I could not object to this, but I could and did object to the odour remaining with me. Have you ever smelt Irish stew after being sixteen hours without food? I say I objected. What I said was: 'Can't you keep that damn stink out of my room?' Landlady said she was sorry; didn't know it annoyed me; but you couldn't keep food from smelling, could you?

So I slammed the door. A little later came a timid tap. I was still lying on the bed, picturing for myself an end in the manner of a youth named Chatterton, but I slithered off to answer the knock. Before I could do so, the door was pushed softly open, and Miss Cork Factory pushed a soft head through it.

'Say, don't mind me, do you? But here, I know all about you. I been watching you, and the old girl's told me, too. She given you notice? Listen. I got a good old stew going in here. More'n enough for two. Come on!'

What would you have done? I was seventeen; and she, I imagine, was about twenty. But a girl of twenty is three times older than a boy of seventeen. She commanded. She mothered. I felt infinitely childlike and absurd. I thought of refusing; but that seemed an idiotic attempt at dignity which would only amuse this very mature young person. To accept seemed to throw away entirely one's masculinity…But she stepped right into the room then, instinctively patting her hair and smoothing herself, and she took me by the arm.

'Look here, now. Don't you go on this silly way; else you'll be a case for the morchery. Noner your nonsense, now. You come right along in.' She flitted back, pulling me with her, to the lit doorway of her room, a yellow oblong of warmth and fragrance… She chucked me into a rickety chair by the dancing fire, and chattered cheerily while she played hostess, and I sat pale and tried to recover dignity in sulky silence.

She played for a moment or so over a large vegetable dish which stood in the fender, and then uprose, with flaming face and straying hair, and set a large plate of real hot stuff before me on the small table. 'There you are, me old University chum!' served as her invitation to the feast. She shot knife, fork, and spoon across the table with a neat shove-ha'p'ny stroke. Bread followed with the same polite service, and then she settled herself, squarely but very prettily, before her own plate, mocking me with twinkling eyes over her raised spoon.

Her grace was terse but adequate: 'Well—here's may God help us as we deserve!' I dipped my spoon, lifted it with shaking hand, my heart bursting to tell the little dear girl what I thought about her, my lips refusing to do anything of the sort; refusing, indeed, to do anything at all; for having got the spoon that far, I tried to swallow the good stuff that was in it, and—well...I...I burst into tears. Yes, I did.

'What the devil—' she jerked. 'Now what the devil's the matter with—Oh, I know. I see.'

'I can't help it,' I hiccuped. 'It's the st-st-st-stew! It's so goo-goo-good!'

'There, that's all right, kid. I know. I been like that. You have a stretch of rotten luck, and you don't get nothing for perhaps a day, and you feel fit to faint, and then at last you get it, and when you got it, can't touch it. Feel all choky, like, don't you? I know. You'll be all right in a minute. Get some more into you!'

I did. And I was all right. I sat by her fire for the rest of the evening, and smoked her cigarettes— twelve for a penny. And we talked; rather good talk, I fancy. As the food warmed me, so I came out of my shell. And gradually the superior motherliness of my hostess disappeared; I was no longer abject under her gaze; I no longer felt like a sheepish schoolboy. I saw her as what she really was—a pale, rather fragile, very girlish girl. We talked torrentially. We broke into one another's sentences without apology. We talked simultaneously. We hurled autobiography at each other....

That was my last week in Kingsland Road; for luck turned, and I found work—of a sort. I left on the Saturday. I parted from her at Cudgett Street corner. I never asked her name; she never asked mine. She just shook hands, and remarked, airily, 'Well, so long, kid. Good luck.'

From *Limehouse Nights*, 1915

Edward Walford on the Foundling Hospital

A basket was hung at the gate of the hospital in London in which the children were deposited, the persons who brought them ringing a bell to give notice to the officers in attendance. In order to forward the 'little innocents' up from the country, a branch of the carrying trade was established, and babies arrived in London in increasing numbers from the most distant parts of the country. Large prices were, in some instances, paid for their conveyance, a fact which more than hints at the position of the parents; and as the carriage was prepaid, there was a strong inducement on the part of the carriers to get rid of their burthens on the way. Many of the infants were drowned; all of them were neglected, and that, in the large majority of cases, was equal to their death. It was publicly asserted in the House of Commons that one man, having the charge of five infants in baskets—they appeared to have been packed like so many sucking-pigs—and happening to get drunk on his journey, lay asleep all night on a common, and in the morning three out of the five were found dead. Many other instances of negligence on the part of carriers, resulting in the death of infants entrusted to them for carriage to London, are on record. Even the clothing in which the children were dressed was often stolen on the way, and the babes were deposited in the basket just as they were born. It is reported that a foundling who lived to become a worthy banker in the north of England, but who was received into the hospital at this time, being in after life anxious to make some inquiry into his origin, applied at the hospital, when all the information he could obtain from this source was that it appeared on the books of the establishment that he was put into the basket at the gate naked.

On the first day of this general reception of infants, June 2nd, 1756, no less than 117 children were deposited in the basket. The easy manner in which the children were thus disposed of led naturally to suspicion, on the part of neighbours, that they had not been fairly dealt with; and a person was actually tried for infanticide, and would have been hung, were it not that he was able to prove that the crime was committed by the carrier. In order to secure the parents against any such suspicion, in 1757 a notice was issued by the governors to the effect, that all persons bringing children should leave some token by which, in case any certificate should be wanted, it might be found out whether such child had been taken into the hospital or not. From that date all the children received had some token attached to their person, and in course of time a goodly collection of these was accumulated. Dr Wynter, in an article on this subject in the *Shilling Magazine*, enumerates several of these tokens, which are still preserved in the hospital. Here are a few of them:—'Coins of an ancient date seem to have been the favourite articles used for this purpose, but there are many things of a more curious nature. A playing card—the ace of hearts—with a dolorous piece of verse written upon it; a ring with two hearts in garnets, broken in half, and then tied together; three or four padlocks, intended, we suppose, as emblems of security; a nut; an ivory fish; an anchor; a gold locket; a lottery ticket. Sometimes a piece of brass, either in the shape of a heart or a crescent moon, was used as a distinguishing mark, generally engraved with some little verse or legend. Thus one has these words upon it, "*In amore hæc sunt vitia*" another has this bit of doggerel:—

"You have my heart;

Though we must part".'

From *Old and New London*, 1878

ON THE STREETS

Burgo Fitzgerald is one of the more endearing characters in Anthony Trollope's 'Palliser' novels (quoted here is an extract from the first in the series, *Can You Forgive Her?*). Well-born but impoverished, he is on the verge of losing his looks and whatever chance he may ever have had of making a good match. He is in love with a beautiful heiress, Lady Glencora M'Cluskie, and even though she is already married to his fabulously rich rival, Plantagenet Palliser, he still believes—and it is a belief rooted in romance rather than opportunism—that there is a chance they may elope. But he needs money. In order to raise it he applies to his unscrupulous friend, George Vavasor. A desperate plot is hatched, involving worthless guarantees and the rapacious Gray's Inn moneylender, Mr Magruin. Relieved, the naive Burgo walks out into the London night, which he brings to an end with a startling and memorably described act of generosity.

Jack London (1876–1916) was a Californian writer and war correspondent, famous for his 1903 bestseller *The Call of the Wild*, the tale of a St Bernard dog called Buck who is forced to exchange an agreeable and incident-free small-town life for the hurly-burly of the Klondike gold rush. In 1902 the author spent several weeks in London's East End. *The People of the Abyss* tells of his experiences and of the many people he warmly engaged with. What marks London's account is the false conviction, held by many foreign visitors to London, that the poor were on the verge of a cataclysmic revolution. Interestingly, the stoicism of the English temperament is something that London seems to miss entirely.

Charles Dickens's description of the life of Jo the Crossing Sweeper from *Bleak House*, says much about his view of society and its feral underclass. The essayist Richard Steele (1672–1729), one of the founders of *The Spectator* magazine, is importuned by a street girl in Covent Garden.

The final extract is a poem by D.H. Lawrence (1885–1930), describing a botched attempt to give money to a destitute woman sleeping rough on the Embankment.

Anthony Trollope's ne'er do well does a good turn to a poor street girl

[Burgo] strove hard to cheat himself into a belief that he would do a good thing in carrying Lady Glen-cora away from her husband. Bad as had been his life he had never before done aught so bad as that. The more fixed his intention became, the more thoroughly he came to perceive how great and grievous was the crime which he contemplated. To elope with another man's wife no longer appeared to him to be a joke at which such men as he might smile. But he tried to think that in this case there would be special circumstances which would almost justify him, and also her. They had loved each other and had sworn to love each other with constancy. There had been no change in the feelings or even in the wishes of either of them. But cold people had come between them with cold calculations, and had separated them. She had been, he told himself, made to marry a man she did not love. If they two loved each other truly, would it not still be better that they should come together? Would not the sin be forgiven on account of the injustice which had been done to them? Had Mr Palliser a right to expect more from a wife who had been made to marry him without loving him? Then he reverted to those dreams of a life of love, in some sunny country, of which he had spoken to Vavasor, and he strove to nourish them. Vavasor had laughed at him, talking of Juan and Haidee. But Vavasor, he said to himself, was a hard cold man, who had no touch of romance in his character. He would not be laughed out of his plan by such as he,—nor would he be frightened by the threat of any Lambro who might come after him, whether he might come in the guise of indignant uncle or injured husband.

He had crossed from Regent Street through Hanover Square, and as he came out by the iron gates into Oxford Street, a poor wretched girl, lightly clad in thin raiment, into whose bones the sharp freezing air was penetrating, asked him for money. Would he give her something to get drink, so that for a moment she might feel the warmth of her life renewed? Such midnight petitions were common enough in his ears, and he was passing on without thinking of her. But she was urgent, and took hold of him. 'For love of God,' she said, 'if it's only a penny to get a glass of gin! Feel my hand,—how cold it is.' And she strove to put it up against his face.

He looked round at her and saw that she was very young,—sixteen, perhaps, at the most, and that she had once,—nay very lately,—been exquisitely pretty. There still lingered about her eyes some remains of that look of perfect innocency and pure faith which had been hers not more than twelve months since. And now, at midnight, in the middle of the streets, she was praying for a pennyworth of gin, as the only comfort she knew, or could expect!

'You are cold!' said he, trying to speak to her cheer-ily.

'Cold!' said she, repeating the word, and striving to wrap herself closer in her rags, as she shivered—'Oh God! if you knew what it was to be as cold as I am! I have nothing in the world,—not one penny,—not a hole to lie in!'

'We are alike then,' said Burgo, with a slight low laugh. 'I also have nothing. You cannot be poorer than I am.'

'You poor!' she said. And then she looked up into his face. 'Gracious; how beautiful you are! Such as you are never poor.'

He laughed again,—in a different tone. He always laughed when any one told him of his beauty. 'I am a deal poorer than you, my girl,' he said. 'You have nothing. I have thirty thousand pounds worse than nothing. But come along, and I will get you some-thing to eat.'

'Will you?' said she, eagerly. Then looking up at him again, she exclaimed—'Oh, you are so handsome!'

He took her to a public-house and gave her bread and meat and beer, and stood by her while she ate it. She was shy with him then, and would fain have taken it to a corner by herself, had he allowed her. He perceived this, and turned his back to her, but still spoke to her a word or two as she ate. The woman at the bar who served him looked at him wonderingly, staring into his face; and the pot-boy woke himself thoroughly that he might look at Burgo; and the waterman from the cab-stand stared at him; and women who came in for gin looked almost lovingly up into his eyes. He regarded them all not at all, showing no feeling of disgrace at his position, and no desire to carry himself as a ruffler. He quietly paid what was due when the girl had finished her meal, and then walked with her out of the shop. 'And now,' said he, 'what must I do with you? If I give you a shilling can you get a bed?' She told him that she could get a bed for sixpence. 'Then keep the other sixpence for your breakfast,' said he. 'But you must promise me that you will buy no gin to-night.' She promised him, and then he gave her his hand as he wished her good night;— his hand, which it had been the dearest wish of Lady Glencora to call her own. She took it and pressed it to her lips. 'I wish I might once see you again,' she said, 'because you are so good and so beautiful.' He laughed again cheerily, and walked on, crossing the street towards Cavendish Square. She stood looking at him till he was out of sight, and then as she moved away,—let us hope to the bed which his bounty had provided, and not to a gin-shop,—she exclaimed to herself again and again—'Gracious, how beautiful he was!'

From *Can You Forgive Her?*, 1865

Jack London on life on the streets

'An' now,' said the sweated one, the 'earty man who worked so fast as to dazzle one's eyes, 'I'll show you one of London's lungs. This is Spitalfields Garden.' And he mouthed the word 'garden' with scorn.

The shadow of Christ's Church falls across Spital- fields Garden, and in the shadow of Christ's Church, at three o'clock in the afternoon, I saw a sight I never wish to see again. There are no flowers in this gar- den, which is smaller than my own rose garden at home. Grass only grows here, and it is surrounded by a sharp-spiked iron fencing, as are all the parks of London Town, so that homeless men and women may not come in at night and sleep upon it.

As we entered the garden, an old woman, between fifty and sixty, passed us, striding with sturdy inten- tion if somewhat rickety action, with two bulky bun- dles, covered with sacking, slung fore and aft upon her. She was a woman tramp, a houseless soul, too independent to drag her failing carcass through the workhouse door. Like the snail, she carried her home with her. In the two sacking-covered bundles were her household goods, her wardrobe, linen, and dear feminine possessions.

We went up the narrow gravelled walk. On the benches on either side arrayed a mass of miserable and distorted humanity, the sight of which would have impelled Doré to more diabolical flights of fancy

than he ever succeeded in achieving. It was a welter
of rags and filth, of all manner of loathsome skin
diseases, open sores, bruises, grossness, indecency,
leering monstrosities, and bestial faces. A chill, raw
wind was blowing, and these creatures huddled there
in their rags, sleeping for the most part, or trying
to sleep. Here were a dozen women, ranging in age
from twenty years to seventy. Next a babe, possibly
of nine months, lying asleep, flat on the hard bench,
with neither pillow nor covering, nor with any one
looking after it. Next half-a-dozen men, sleeping bolt
upright or leaning against one another in their sleep.
In one place a family group, a child asleep in its sleeping mother's arms, and the husband (or male mate)
clumsily mending a dilapidated shoe. On another
bench a woman trimming the frayed strips of her rags
with a knife, and another woman, with thread and
needle, sewing up rents. Adjoining, a man holding a
sleeping woman in his arms. Farther on, a man, his
clothing caked with gutter mud, asleep, with head in
the lap of a woman, not more than twenty-five years
old, and also asleep.

It was this sleeping that puzzled me. Why were
nine out of ten of them asleep or trying to sleep? But
it was not till afterwards that I learned. *It is a law of the
powers that be that the homeless shall not sleep by night.*
On the pavement, by the portico of Christ's Church,
where the stone pillars rise toward the sky in a stately

row, were whole rows of men lying asleep or drows-ing, and all too deep sunk in torpor to rouse or be made curious by our intrusion.

From *The People of the Abyss*, 1903

Charles Dickens on Jo the crossing sweeper

It must be a strange state to be like Jo! To shuffle through the streets, unfamiliar with the shapes, and in utter darkness as to the meaning, of those mys-terious symbols, so abundant over the shops, and at the corners of streets, and on the doors, and in the windows! To see people read, and to see peo-ple write, and to see the postmen deliver letters, and not to have the least idea of all that language—to be, to every scrap of it, stone blind and dumb! It must be very puzzling to see the good company going to the churches on Sundays, with their books in their hands, and to think (for perhaps Jo DOES think at odd times) what does it all mean, and if it means any-thing to anybody, how comes it that it means nothing to me? To be hustled, and jostled, and moved on; and really to feel that it would appear to be perfectly true that I have no business here, or there, or anywhere; and yet to be perplexed by the consideration that I AM here somehow, too, and everybody overlooked me until I became the creature that I am! It must be a strange state, not merely to be told that I am scarcely human…but to feel it of my own knowledge all my life! To see the horses, dogs, and cattle go by me and to know that in ignorance I belong to them and not to the superior beings in my shape, whose delicacy I offend! Jo's ideas of a criminal trial, or a judge, or a bishop, or a government, or that inestimable jewel to him (if he only knew it) the Constitution, should be strange! His whole material and immaterial life is wonderfully strange; his death, the strangest thing of all. Jo comes out of Tom-all-Alone's [his slum lodging], meeting the tardy morning which is always late in getting down there, and munches his dirty bit of bread as he comes along. His way lying through many streets, and the houses not yet being open, he sits down to breakfast on the door-step of the Society for the Propagation of the Gospel in Foreign Parts and gives it a brush when he has finished as an acknowledgment of the accommodation. He admires the size of the edifice and wonders what it's all about. He has no idea, poor wretch, of the spiritual destitution of a coral reef in the Pacific or what it costs to look up the precious souls among the coco-nuts and bread-fruit. He goes to his crossing and begins to lay it out for the day. The town awakes; the great tee-totum is set up for its daily spin and whirl; all that unaccountable reading and writing, which has been suspended for a few hours, recommences. Jo and the other lower animals get on in the unintelligible mess as they can. It is market-day. The blinded oxen, over-goaded, over-driven, never guided, run into wrong places and are beaten out, and plunge red-eyed and foaming at stone walls, and often sorely hurt the innocent, and often sorely hurt themselves. Very like Jo and his order; very, very like! A band of music comes and plays. Jo listens to it. So does a dog—a drover's dog, waiting for his master outside a butcher's shop, and evidently thinking about those sheep he has had upon his mind for some hours and is happily rid of. He seems perplexed respecting three or four, can't remember where he left them, looks up and down the street as half expecting to see them astray, suddenly pricks up his ears and remembers all about it. A thoroughly vagabond dog, accustomed to low company and public- houses; a terrific dog to sheep, ready at a whistle to scamper over their backs and tear out mouthfuls of their wool; but an educated, improved, developed dog who has been taught his duties and knows how to discharge them. He and Jo listen to the music, probably with much the same amount of animal satisfaction; likewise as to awakened association, aspiration, or regret, melancholy or joyful reference to things beyond the senses, they are probably upon a par. But, otherwise, how far above the human listener is the brute! Turn that dog's descendants wild, like Jo, and in a very few years they will so degenerate that they will lose even their bark—but not their bite.

From *Bleak House*, 1853

Richard Steele meets a street girl

The other evening, passing along near Covent Garden, I was jogged on the elbow as I turned into the Piazza…by a slim young girl of about seventeen, who with a pert air asked me if I was for a pint of wine… We stood under one of the arches by twilight; and there I could observe as exact features as I had ever seen, the most agreeable shape, the finest neck and bosom, in a word the whole person of a woman exquisitely beautiful. She affected to allure me with a forced wantonness in her look and air; but I saw it checked with hunger and cold: her eyes were wan and eager, her dress thin and tawdry, her mien genteel and childish. This strange figure gave me much anguish of heart, and to avoid being seen with her went away, but could not forbear giving her a crown. The poor thing sighed, curtseyed, and with a sigh, expressed with the utmost vehemence, turned from me. This creature is what they call newly come upon the town, but who, I suppose, falling into cruel hands, was left in the first month from her dishonour, and exposed to pass through the hands and discipline of one of those hags of Hell whom we call bawds.

From *The Spectator*, 1712

D.H. Lawrence: *Charity* (1916)

By the river

In the black wet night as the furtive rain slinks down,

Dropping and starting from sleep
Alone on a seat
A woman crouches.

I must go back to her.

I want to give her
Some money. Her hand slips out of the breast
                                    of her gown
Asleep. My fingers creep
Carefully over the sweet
Thumb-mound, into the palm's deep pouches.

So, the gift!

God, how she starts!
And looks at me, and looks in the palm of her hand!
And again at me!
I turn and run
Down the Embankment, run for my life.

But why?—why?

Because of my heart's
Beating like sobs, I come to myself, and stand
In the street spilled over splendidly
With wet, flat lights. What I've done
I know not, my soul is in strife.

The touch was on the quick. I want to forget.

ADDICTION

Vice in the forms of gambling and drug addiction has always bedevilled and enlivened city life. Many of the best known London clubs such as White's and Brooks's drew their life's blood from the premise that a dedicated gambler will bet on anything. An instance of this compulsive attitude is related by Captain Gronow (*see p. 204*), concerning Lord Byron's supposed shooting skills. Gronow and several other of the best shots in London would assemble at a gun club, Manton's Shooting Gallery, and bet on the outcome of their marksmanship. Gronow, a crack pistol shot, usually won but Byron also had a good eye and was a bad loser: 'Wedderburn Webster was present when the poet, intensely delighted with his own skill, boasted to Joe Manton that he considered himself the best shot in London. "No, my lord," replied Manton, "not the best; but your shooting, to-day, was respectable;" upon which Byron waxed wroth, and left the shop in a violent passion.' The high-rollers at cards were vividly chronicled by Gronow, men such as General Scott, the father-in-law of George Canning, and the Duke of Portland, who was known to have won £200,000 at White's thanks to his 'notorious sobriety'. Today, the card room at Brooks's, elegantly restored by the politician Alan Clark, is still the scene of elegant ebbs and flows of fortune, usually at backgammon.

The two next scenes are from the high and low end of London gambling life. 'Dinner at Blades' is a memorable chapter in Ian Fleming's *Moonraker* in which James Bond and his MI6 controller, 'M', plot the downfall of the Liverpudlian arch-villain Hugo Drax, who has been cheating at cards at M's exclusive club. Ian Fleming (1908–64) was an Intelligence officer working in Room 39 of the Admiralty, a department of MI6 reserved for high-powered linguists and administrators. To his eternal regret he never saw service 'in the field' and it is fair to say that Bond was something of an entertaining alter ego for him, a way of working out his frustrations. The atmosphere of the club is exquisitely observed and Bond's outrageous preparations for his head-to-head with Drax (an inspiring tonic of Benzedrine washed down with champagne and vodka whilst eyeing up the club waitress) are observed with an absence of political correctness unthinkable today.

In stark contrast to this plutocratic scene, Alexander Baron's compulsive East End Jewish gambler, Harry Boas, visits his brother-in-law Gus in Finchley. Baron (1917–99) is perhaps one of the most underrated London novelists of the post-war period. *The Lowlife*, from which this extract is taken, is an absorbing account of Harry's gambling habit and his attempts to achieve some form of redemption through tolerance of and generosity to some of the misfits who come in and out of his life in Hackney.

Drugs are another addiction. Opium was legally available in two forms in 19th-century Britain, laudanum
and raw opium resin, both highly addictive. Laudanum was sold as a medicine either in pill form or as
a liquid solution of opium, alcohol and bitter herbs.
Opium resin was the disreputable alternative, used by
hardened reprobates as a recreational drug and smoked
in pipes or tainted cigarettes, often in the opium dens
of London's East End. Supplies of opium were cheap
and plentiful. Its cultivation had been successfully mo-
nopolised by the British East India Company and the
Anglo-Chinese Opium Wars of 1839–42 and 1856–60,
occasioned by the Qing dynasty's unsuccessful attempts
to prevent Britain exporting opium to China, had little
lasting effect on the opium trade or on its consumption
in Britain. A more enduring legacy was the myth that
London opium dens were exclusively run by Chinese
immigrants. In reality, the small cluster of opium dens
around Limehouse was run by a motley confederation
of native Londoners, Chinese, Indians and Lascars. The
Lascars—swarthy sailors from the subcontinent of India and all points east—became a stock type in crime
fiction that endured well into the late 20th century.

The opium den is as much a part of London's my-
thology as it is of its history, an offshoot of Oriental-
ism that was profitably exploited by leading authors,
as the extracts from Dickens, Wilde and Conan Doyle

demonstrate. The central character in *The Mystery of Edwin Drood*, Dickens's last and unfinished novel, is John Jasper, the choirmaster of a provincial cathedral, who leads a double life as an opium addict.

After a visit to an opium den, Wilde's Dorian Gray narrowly escapes retribution in the lamplight of a Limehouse alley when confronted by the brother of a young actress he had betrayed and who committed suicide. He is saved by his eternal and unfading youth, a gift obtained through a dark, supernatural pact that has him remain young while his portrait ages in his place. He cannot possibly be the same man that the brother imagines.

Whilst the evils of opium dens may have been subject to literary exaggeration, laudanum abuse was a very real social phenomenon. Thanks to its tax-free status as a medication, laudanum had for a time been the favoured intoxicant of the poor, a bottle of it being somewhat cheaper than a bottle of gin towards the end of the 18th century. By the end of the Regency, apothecaries had developed innumerable proprietary brands and marketed them as catch-all remedies for a variety of disorders including gout, muscle pain, menstrual problems and sleeplessness. The educated middle class was drawn into a dependency on the drug, in much the same way that their latter-day counterparts fell victims to tranquilliser addiction in the late decades of the 20th century. Elizabeth Barrett Browning and Wilkie Collins both became addicted. The novelist Hall Caine (1853–1931) described Collins, who first took laudanum to alleviate the pain of gout and rheumatism, drinking it by the wineglass in an attempt 'to stimulate the brain and steady the nerves'. Elizabeth Barrett Browning found temporary deliverance from the intense pain of spinal tuberculosis, from which she had suffered since childhood. As long as the trance-like interludes of release lasted, she had nothing but praise for the drug. 'I am writing such poems—allegorical—philosophical—poetical—ethical—synthetically arranged! I am in a fit of writing—could write all day & night—and long to live by myself for three months in a forest of chestnuts & cedars, in an hourly succession of poetical paragraphs & morphine draughts.' (Elizabeth Barrett Browning, to her brother, 1843.) Later, as her dependency on the drug increased, the forest of chestnuts disappeared, as did the poppy field mirages that had sometimes brightened her letters to Robert. The side-effects were dire and Elizabeth suffered a miscarriage and other distressing complications.

The two best-known literary opium addicts, Samuel Taylor Coleridge and Thomas de Quincey, were inveterate consumers of laudanum. At the height of his addiction, Coleridge consumed two quarts every week, supplied by his doctor, Aaron Potter. Dr Potter, Thomas de Quincey suggested, may well have been the mysterious 'Man from Porlock' who famously interrupted the composition of *Kubla Khan*. De Quincey routinely bought his laudanum from a 'druggist', the equivalent of today's chemist. *His Confessions of an English Opium-Eater* (1821) is remarkable for its descriptions of the effects of the drug. Perhaps the most disturbing effect described—and one that is reprised in many fictional accounts of opium consumption—is the extent to which the drug plays havoc with the addict's perception of the world around him:

> 'The sense of space, and in the end, the sense of time, were both powerfully affected. Buildings, landscapes, &c. were exhibited in proportions so vast as the bodily eye is not fitted to conceive. Space swelled, and was amplified to an extent of unutterable infinity. This, however, did not disturb me so much as the vast expansion of time; I sometimes seemed to have lived for 70 or 100 years in one night; nay, sometimes had feelings representative of a millennium passed in that time, or, however, of a duration far beyond the limits of any human experience.'

There are no opium dens to be found in Limehouse today, though trust-funded neo-Dorian aristocrats of Faustian persuasion may sometimes be found striking deals with the drug dealers of Tower Hamlets.

Dinner at Blades

It was eight o'clock as Bond followed M through the tall doors, across the well of the staircase from the card room, that opened into the beautiful white and gold Regency dining-room of Blades.

M chose not to hear a call from Basildon who was presiding over the big centre table where there were still two places vacant. Instead, he walked firmly across the room to the end one of a row of six smaller tables, waved Bond into the comfortable armed chair that faced outwards into the room, and himself took the one on Bond's left so that his back was to the company.

The head steward was already behind Bond's chair. He placed a broad menu card beside his plate and handed another to M. 'Blades' was written in fine gold script across the top. Below there was a forest of print.

'Don't bother to read through all that,' said M, 'unless you've got no ideas. One of the first rules of the club, and one of the best, was that any member may speak for any dish, cheap or dear, but he must pay for it. The same's true today, only the odds are one doesn't have to pay for it. Just order what you feel like.' He looked up at the steward. 'Any of that Beluga caviar left, Porterfield?'

'Yes, sir. There was a new delivery last week.'

'Well,' said M, 'Caviar for me. Devilled kidney and a slice of your excellent bacon. Peas and new potatoes.

Strawberries in kirsch. What about you, James?'

'I've got a mania for really good smoked salmon,' said Bond. Then he pointed down the menu. 'Lamb; cutlets. The same vegetables as you, as it's May. Asparagus with Bearnaise sauce sounds wonderful. And perhaps a slice of pineapple.' He sat back and pushed the menu away.

'Thank heaven for a man who makes up his mind,' said M. He looked up at the steward. 'Have you got all that, Porterfield?'

'Yes, sir.' The steward smiled. 'You wouldn't care for a marrow bone after the strawberries, sir? We got half a dozen in today from the country, and I'd specially kept one in case you came in.'

'Of course. You know I can't resist them. Bad for me but it can't be helped. God knows what I'm celebrating this evening. But it doesn't often happen. Ask Grimley to come over, would you?'

'He's here now, sir,' said the steward, making way for the wine-waiter.

'Ah, Grimley, some vodka, please.' He turned to Bond. 'Not the stuff you had in your cocktail. This is real pre-war Wolfschmidt from Riga. Like some with your smoked salmon?'

'Very much,' said Bond.

'Then what?' asked M. 'Champagne? Personally I'm going to have a half-bottle of claret. The Mouton Rothschild '34, please, Grimley. But don't pay any at-

tention to me, James. I'm an old man. Champagne's
no good for me. We've got some good champagnes,
haven't we, Grimley? None of that stuff you're always
telling me about, I'm afraid, James. Don't often see it
in England. Taittinger, wasn't it?'

Bond smiled at M's memory. 'Yes,' he said, 'but it's
only a fad of mine. As a matter of fact, for various reasons I believe I would like to drink champagne this
evening. Perhaps I could leave it to Grimley.'

The wine-waiter was pleased. 'If I may suggest it,
sir, the Dom Perignon '46. I understand that France
only sells it for dollars, sir, so you don't often see it in
London. I believe it .was a gift from the Regency Club
in New York, sir. I have some on ice at the moment.
It's the Chairman's favourite and he's told me to have
it ready every evening in case he needs it.'

Bond smiled his agreement.

'So be it, Grimley,' said M. The Dom Perignon.
Bring it straight away, would you?'

A waitress appeared and put racks of fresh toast on
the table and a silver dish of Jersey butter. As she bent
over the table her black skirt brushed Bond's arm and
he looked up into two pert, sparkling eyes under a
soft fringe of hair. The eyes held his for a fraction
of a second and then she whisked away. Bond's eyes
followed the white bow at her waist and the starched
collar and cuffs of her uniform as she went down the
long room. His eyes narrowed. He recalled a pre-war-

establishment in Paris where the girls were dressed with the same exciting severity. Until they turned round and showed their backs. He smiled to himself. The *Marthe Richards* law had changed all that.

M turned from studying their neighbours behind him. 'Why were you so cryptic about drinking champagne?'

'Well, if you don't mind, sir,' Bond explained, 'I've got to get a bit tight tonight. I'll have to seem very drunk when the time comes. It's not an easy thing to act unless you do it with a good deal of conviction. I hope you won't get worried if I seem to get frayed at the edges later on.'

M shrugged his shoulders. 'You've got a head like a rock, James,' he said. 'Drink as much as you like if it's going to help. Ah, here's the vodka.'

When M poured him three fingers from the frosted carafe Bond took a pinch of black pepper and dropped it on the surface of the vodka. The pepper slowly settled to the bottom of the glass leaving a few grains on the surface which Bond dabbed up with the tip of a finger. Then he tossed the cold liquor well to the back of his throat and put his glass, with the dregs of the pepper at the bottom, back on the table.

M gave him a glance of rather ironical inquiry.

'It's a trick the Russians taught me that time you attached me to the Embassy in Moscow,' apologized

Bond. 'There's often quite a lot of fusel oil on the surface of this stuff—at least there used to be when it was badly distilled. Poisonous. In Russia, where you get a lot of bath-tub liquor, it's an understood thing to sprinkle a little pepper in your glass. It takes the fusel oil to the bottom. I got to like the taste and now it's a habit. But I shouldn't have insulted the club Wolfschmidt,' he added with a grin.

M grunted. 'So long as you don't put pepper in Basildon's favourite champagne,' he said drily.

A harsh bray of laughter came from a table at the far end of the room. M looked over his shoulder and then turned back to his caviar.

'What do you think of this man Drax?' he said through a mouthful of buttered toast.

Bond helped himself to another slice of smoked salmon from the silver dish beside him. It had the delicate glutinous texture only achieved by Highland curers—very different from the desiccated products of Scandinavia. He rolled a wafer-thin slice of brown bread-and-butter into a cylinder and contemplated it thoughtfully.

'One can't like his manner much. At first I was rather surprised that you tolerate him here.' He glanced at M, who shrugged his shoulders. 'But that's none of my business and anyway clubs would be very dull without a sprinkling of eccentrics. And in any case he's a national hero and a millionaire and obviously an adequate card-player. Even when he isn't helping himself to the odds,' he added. 'But I can see he's the sort of man I always imagined. Full-blooded, ruthless, shrewd. Plenty of guts. I'm not surprised he's managed to get where he is. What I don't understand is why he should be quite happy to throw it all away. This cheating of his. It's really beyond belief. What's he trying to prove with it? That he can beat everyone at everything? He seems to put so much passion into his cards—as if it wasn't a game at all, but some sort of trial of strength. You've only got to look at his fingernails. Bitten to the quick. And he sweats too much. There's a lot of tension there somewhere. It comes out in those ghastly jokes of his. They're harsh. There's no light touch about them. He seemed to want to squash Basildon like a fly. Hope I shall be able to keep my temper. That manner of his is pretty riling. He even treats his partner as if he was muck. He hasn't quite got under my skin, but I shan't at all mind sticking a very sharp pin in him tonight.' He smiled at M. 'If it comes off, that is.'

'I know what you, mean,' said M. 'But you may be being a bit hard on the man. After all, it's a big step from the Liverpool docks, or wherever he came from, to where he is now. And he's one of those people who was born with naturally hairy heels. Nothing to do with snobbery. I expect his mates in Liverpool found him just as loud-mouthed as Blades does. As for his cheating, there's probably a crooked streak in him somewhere. I dare say he took plenty of short cuts on his way up. Somebody said that to become very rich you have to be helped by a combination of remarkable circumstances and an unbroken run of luck. It certainly isn't only the qualities of people that make them rich. At least that's my experience. At the beginning, getting together the first ten thousand, or the first hundred thousand, things have got to go damn right. And in that commodity business after the war, with all the regulations and restrictions, I expect it was often a case of being able to drop a thousand pounds in the right pocket. Officials. The ones who understand nothing but addition, division—and silence. The useful ones.'

M paused while the next course came. With it arrived the champagne in a silver ice-bucket, and the small wicker-basket containing M's half-bottle of claret

The wine-steward waited until they had delivered a favourable judgement on the wines and then moved away. As he did so a page came up to their table. 'Commander Bond?' he asked.

Bond took the envelope that was handed to him and slit it open. He took out a thin paper packet and carefully opened it under the level of the table. It contained a white powder. He took a silver fruit knife off the table and dipped the tip of the blade into the packet so that about half its contents were transferred to the knife. He reached for his glass of champagne and tipped the powder into it.

'Now what?' said M with a trace of impatience.

There was no hint of apology in Bond's face. It wasn't M who was going to have to do the work that evening. Bond knew what he was doing. Whenever he had a job of work to do he would take infinite pains beforehand and leave as little as possible to chance. then if something went wrong it was the unforeseeable. For that he accepted no responsibility.

'Benzedrine,' he said. 'I rang up my secretary before dinner and asked her to wangle some out of the surgery at Headquarters. It's what I shall need if I'm to keep my wits about me tonight. It's apt to make one feel a bit overconfident, but that'll be a help too.' He stirred the champagne with a scrap of toast so that the white powder whirled among the bubbles. Then he drank the mixture down with one long swallow. 'It doesn't taste,' said Bond, 'and the champagne is quite excellent.'

M smiled at him indulgently. 'It's your funeral,' he said. 'Now we'd better get on with our dinner. How were the cutlets?'

'Superb,' said Bond. 'I could cut them with a fork. The best English cooking is the best in the world— particularly at this time of year. By the way, what stakes will we be playing for this evening? I don't mind very much. We ought to end up the winners. But I'd like to know how much it will cost Drax.'

'Drax likes to play for what he calls "One and One",' said M, helping himself from the strawberries that had just been put on the table. 'Modest sounding stake, if you don't know what it stands for. In fact it's one tenner a hundred and one hundred pounds on the rubber.'

'Oh,' said Bond respectfully. 'I see.'

'But he's perfectly happy to play for Two and Two or even Three and Three. Mounts up at those figures. The average rubber of bridge at Blades is about ten points: That's zoo at One and One. And the bridge here makes for big rubbers. There are no conventions so there's plenty of gambling and bluffing. Sometimes it's more like poker. They're a mixed lot of players. Some of them are the best in England, but others are terribly wild. Don't seem to mind how much they lose. General Bealey, just behind us.' M made a gesture with his head. 'Doesn't know the reds from the blacks. Nearly always a few hundred down at the end of the week. Doesn't seem to care. Bad heart. No dependants. Stacks of money from jute. But Duff Sutherland, the scruffy-looking chap next to the chairman, is an absolute killer. Makes a regular ten thousand a year out of the club. Nice chap. Wonderful card manners. Used to play chess for England.'

M was interrupted by the arrival of his marrow bone. It was placed upright in a spotless lace napkin on the silver plate. An ornate silver marrow-scoop was laid beside it.

After the asparagus, Bond had little appetite for the thin slivers of pineapple. He tipped the last of the ice-cold champagne into his glass. He felt wonderful. The effects of the benzedrine and champagne had more than offset the splendour of the food. For the first time he took his mind away from the dinner and his conversation with M and glanced round the room.

It was a sparkling scene. There were perhaps fifty men in the room, the majority in dinner jackets, all at ease with themselves and their surroundings, all stimulated by the peerless food and drink, all animated by a common interest — the prospect of high gambling, the grand slam, the ace pot, the key-throw in a 64 game at backgammon. There might be cheats or possible cheats amongst them, men who beat their wives, men with perverse instincts, greedy men, cowardly men, lying men; but the elegance of the room invested each one with a kind of aristocracy.

At the far end, above the cold table, laden with lobsters, pies, joints and delicacies in aspic, Romney's unfinished full-length portrait of Mrs Fitzherbert gazed provocatively across at Fragonard's

Jeu de Cartes, the broad conversation-piece which half-filled the opposite wall above the Adam fireplace. Along the lateral walls, in the centre of each gilt-edged panel, was one of the rare engravings of the Hell-Fire Club in which each figure is shown making a minute gesture of scatological or magical significance. Above, marrying the walls into the ceiling, ran a frieze in plaster relief of carved urns and swags interrupted at intervals by the capitals of the fluted pilasters which framed the windows and the tall double doors, the latter delicately carved with a design showing the Tudor Rose interwoven with a ribbon effect.

The central chandelier, a cascade of crystal ropes terminating in a broad basket of strung quartz, sparkled warmly above the white damask tablecloths and George IV silver. Below, in the centre of each table, branched candlesticks distributed the golden light of three candles, each surmounted by a red silk shade, so that the faces of the diners shone with a convivial warmth which glossed over the occasional chill of an eye or cruel twist of a mouth.

Even as Bond drank in the warm elegance of the scene, some of the groups began to break up. There was a drift towards the door accompanied by an exchange of challenges, side-bets, and exhortations to hurry up and get down to business. Sir Hugo Drax, his hairy red face shining with cheerful anticipation, came towards them with Meyer in his wake.

'Well, gentlemen,' he said jovially as he reached their table. 'Are the lambs ready for the slaughter and the geese for the plucking?' He grinned and in wolfish pantomime drew a finger across his throat. We'll go ahead and lay out the axe and the basket. Made your wills?'

'Be with you in a moment,' said M edgily. 'You go along and stack the cards.'

Drax laughed. 'We shan't need any artificial aids,' he said. 'Don't be long.' He turned and made for the door. Meyer enveloped them in an uncertain smile and followed him.

M grunted. 'We'll have coffee and brandy in the card room,' he said to Bond. 'Can't smoke here. Now then. Any final plans?'

'I'll have to fatten him up for the kill, so please don't worry if I seem to be getting high,' said Bond. 'We'll just have to play our normal game till the time comes. When it's his deal, we'll have to be careful. Of course, he can't alter the cards and there's no reason why he shouldn't deal us good hands, but he's bound to bring off some pretty remarkable coups. Do you mind if I sit on his left?'

'No,' said M. 'Anything else?'

Bond reflected for a moment. 'Only one thing, sir,' he said. When the time comes, I shall take a white handkerchief out of my coat pocket. That will mean that you are about to be dealt a Yarborough. Would you please leave the bidding of that hand to me?'

From *Moonraker* by Ian Fleming, 1954

Alexander Baron's compulsive gambler

My name is Harryboy Boas. (Bo-as, two syllables, please.) At the moment I have thirty pounds in the world. But I face the future with confidence. The dogs are running at White City tonight. In the third there is an animal, which, I heard this morning... Ah, I should have such luck. But a man can dream. I bother no-one.

My story starts one night last year. It didn't seem a night different from any other. We are carried to the grave on a stream of dead days and nights. We live them and forget them. Yet who knows on which dead day or night a terrible change can come into a life? A disease starts. The seeds of a crisis, a disaster, a great joy, are sown. At the time we are aware of nothing. I didn't know that night. I went round to my sister Debbie. How could I know what was coming to me?

Debbie lives in Finchley, the smart part. Finchley, as few people know, is one of the millionaire quarters of London. There are roads in Finchley that make Kensington look poor. Houses at forty thousand, three-car garages (Rolls, sonny's Jag and mummy's shopping Dauphine), driveways, grounds front and rear, and butlers. Not that Debbie married so high. A

fifteen-thousand-pound house and a Spanish couple
to look after it is all she's got, poor girl. All right, so
she hasn't done so bad. When she married Gus in the
third year of the war, he was a boy without money,
only a medical certificate to say the army didn't want
him, and an ambition to make a book. So a book he
made, and in a modest way, he hasn't done so badly.
When did a bookie starve?

He is a good fellow, Gus. He didn't marry Deb for
her money. Money in our family. Nor for her good
looks. Debbie was always a fat girl, with a face so
helpless and gentle it breaks your heart. He was fond
of her. He liked the girl. It happens sometimes…

I went round there that night, and not a bad word
was said till after supper. This is a big point for Gus.
I told you, he is a good man. Life Governor of hospitals. A name for generosity. He grunts something that
sounds like a greeting, goes behind the bar (this is a
semi-circular bar, all glass in front, lit from beneath,
with richly-coloured Venetian glasses on shelves. Very
pretty. Behind the barman are the shelves of bottles,
and behind the bottles is a big mirror) and pours me a
whisky that would knock down a carthorse. He gives
it to me, picks up his own and says, 'Cheers.' That's all.
He must have been bursting, but he kept his anger in.

Debbie, dear Debbie, just comes out into the hall.
The servant opens the door, and Debbie always
comes out and hovers timidly behind her. I know

how frightened she must be of those servants, even after all these years. She gives me her big sad smile and says straight away, 'I've got lutkas on, Harryboy.'

Gus grunts, 'What you like, she cooks. When you come, I eat well.'

'Other times you starve?' I say. 'Where did you get that belly?'

'I'm down to my right weight,' he says. 'Ten years' time you should be as flat as me here.' He smacks his belly.

Debbie says, 'He plays squash two nights a week. It kills him.' She has a Benedictine. She always goes for sweet liqueurs.

So for supper we have potato lutkas, soup with meat balls and thin vermicelli, a half a chicken each with roast potatoes, sweet corn and cream spinach (the old folk, rest their souls, used to be Orthodox, but Gus and Debbie keep a modern home), and in case I'm hungry afterwards, Debbie brings out a big apple tart, with fruit salad and cream to finish. I ought to mention that we had a good white wine, at the right temperature. You think a bookmaker has to be a fat ignoramus? Gus knows all about wines, even if he hasn't got a butler. All the time, not a bad word.

After supper we are back in the lounge, and puffing our Havanas, and the storm breaks.

Gus looks at the ash on his cigar and starts quietly, as if he is delivering a stage soliloquy. 'A schlemiel I've got for a brother-in-law. A half-wit. A lunatic. A good wife I marry, and she has to have the village idiot for a brother. Can good ever come to a man without trouble?'

I keep dumb, breathe cigar smoke round myself. Now he addresses himself to me. 'Couldn't you do what I told you? Couldn't you leave well alone? For thirty years you been going to the tracks, don't you know when to call it a day? You were so greedy all of a sudden? You thought you were a genius? The prophet Elijah? You were getting your tips from the Almighty?'

Now he starts to lose his temper. He bangs his fist on his chest. 'From me you got the tip. Not the Almighty. Why should the Almighty care about you? A lowlife like you? Did you ever pay a subscription to a synagogue? At least I've got a seat, you should know what I pay for it. You? An atheist, I suppose. Go on, tell me you're an atheist.'

'I'm not an atheist.'

'A discussion now we're having about religion. Thank you. The intellectual. Thank you very much. Who's talking about religion? I'm talking about a tip. I tipped you a dog. It wasn't a gamble. What do I have to teach you at your time of life? It was a fix. The race was fixed. All you had to do was collect the money and go home. Go home, do you hear me? With the money in your pocket. My family, I do it for you because you're my family, my wife's brother, a tip like that I would never give to anyone, a fix you don't talk about. If they pulled my nails out...'

Does it matter what he said next? When the words are unwelcome, I can shut my ears up, curl up inside myself where it's nice and cosy, and dream. I dreamed.

From *The Lowlife*, 1963

In an East London opium den

Only such of the public as are accustomed to read the police news in the daily papers can form any idea as to the kind of place Bluegate Fields is. Commonly it is known as 'Tiger Bay'; on account of the number of ferocious she-creatures in petticoats that lurk and lair there. It is a narrow lane opening on to High Street, Shadwell, at one end, and St George's Street at the other. To the left and right of the narrow lane are many villainous courts and alleys, consisting of one-storey high hovels, each one accommodating as many lodgers as might reasonably occupy an eight-roomed house. The inhabitants of Bluegate Fields are the worst in England, consisting of man-trappers for the shipping lying in the river just below, and the tigress-es before mentioned, who inveigle tipsy sailors from the many surrounding abominable dens 'licensed for dancing and music,' and drug them and strip and rob and ill use them, and pickpockets and coiners and robbers of every degree....It is a fact that while I was inquiring at a public-house for the address of Chi Ki, the Chinaman, I overheard two women at the bar discussing a murderous assault that had happened in the 'Fields' that morning....I was lucky in calling at the public-house where the two women were, since on inquiry I discovered that it was to this place that Chi Ki had directed all letters from his numerous friends. I was glad to find that the barmaid spoke of the opium master in a very respectful manner, calling him Mr Chi Ki. She happened to know, moreover, that the distinguished Chinaman was from home; so I left with her a message for him to the effect that if it accorded with Mr Chi Ki's convenience, a gentleman would be glad to meet him on business at that hostelry at six o'clock the following evening.

He was punctual. Precisely as the clock marked six he put his head in at the door. 'Mr Chi Ki, here's your gentleman,' called out the obliging barmaid, and the Chinaman's body followed his head, and he came towards me bowing low and rubbing his hands. I must confess that I was disappointed at Chi Ki's appearance. Being so celebrated a character, with lords and marquises for his patrons and customers, I expected to see a man able and willing to demonstrate in his attire his native ideas of splendour. It would not have surprised me if so exalted a personage as an opium master had appeared dressed in a gown of gold-embroidered crimson silk, and with a sash and curly-toed slippers; but poor Chi Ki was very poorly

clad indeed. He is a man of ostlerish cut, wearing a
long jacket and a comforter wisped round his neck,
and tight trousers, and an old cloth cap on his head.
He is lame of a leg, too, as many ostlers are. In a few
words I explained my business, and without betray-
ing the least astonishment at its nature he expressed
his readiness to conduct me to his house there and
then.

We went a little way into Bluegate Fields and then
turned into the arched way of an alley, a trifle higher,
maybe, but not nearly so wide as an ordinary coal
cellar doorway. It was as dark as any coal-cellar.
'Come along, sir,' said Chi Ki encouragingly, in his
pigeon English. 'It is down at the bottom and turn
round the corner; come along.'

We arrived at the bottom, and came on a tiny
square of ill-looking little houses and an appalling
odour of bad drainage, and Chi Ki guided me to a
house in a corner as his. It was no larger than the rest
and scarcely as good looking, on account of its many
fractured window-panes and the rough-and-ready
measures that had been resorted to to block out the
wind. Pushing open the outer door, Chi Ki called at
the foot of the stairs for a light. While we waited for
it I peeped into the parlour, which was dark except
for a little blinking fire in an iron skillet, crouching
over which was a Chinaman, looking the picture of
despair, with his knees supporting his arms and his

head resting on his hands, and his pigtail slewed to the fore and projecting over his forehead as a unicorn wears his horn. I observed, too, that there was in the room a large bedstead, with a bed made the wrong way on it

It was an English voice that responded to Chi Ki's demand for a light; and presently a youngish woman, very thin and pale-looking, and scarcely as tidy as she might have been, made her appearance above with a tallow candle in her hand, and politely invited me to walk up. We walked up, and at once came in full view of the renowned opium master's public smoking-room, which served likewise for his private sitting-room and his private bedroom, and, judging from the handle of a saucepan and a suspicion of dirty plates under the bed, for his kitchen as well.

It was an extremely mean and miserable little room. The fireplace was very narrow, and the stove of the ancient narrow-waisted pattern. There was no fender. In the centre of the room was a small round table, and there were three wooden chairs. The chief and most conspicuous article of furniture the room contained was a large four-post bedstead, and a bed like the one downstairs. The bed was not arranged according to the English fashion. It was rolled up bol-ster-wise all along the length of the bedstead, leaving the mattress bare except for a large mat of Chinese grass. The bed-hangings were of some light Chinese gauze, but very dirty, and hitched up slatternly on the hanging-rails. The walls of the room were hung with a few tawdry pictures highly coloured, and contrasting grimly with the blackened walls, all stained above with rain-leakage, and below with the filthy saliva with which the smokers had besprinkled them. The ceiling was as black as the walls, and just over the window there had been an extensive fall of plaster, showing the laths, like grinning teeth in an ugly mouth.

There was a customer waiting, which at once gave Chi Ki an opportunity for displaying the mysteries of his craft. The preparations for enjoying the luxury of opium smoking were curious enough. Chi Ki's first move was to spread a piece of cloth on the mat that covered the mattress. Then he brought out a small common oil lamp and lit it and placed it in the centre of the piece of cloth. Next he produced a small box containing his smoking tools, and finally a little gallipot and an instrument like a flute, with a wooden cup with a lid to it screwed on at a distance of about three inches from the end. It was not a flute, however, but a pipe,—the pipe. As the customer caught sight of the odd-looking implement (he was quite a young man and more respectable-looking than Chi Ki himself) he licked his lips, and his eyes glistened like those of the domestic feline creature when it hears the welcome cry that announces its dinner. I asked permission to examine the pipe. It was simply an eighteen-inch length of yellow bamboo with the cup of dark-coloured baked clay before mentioned fitted into a sort of spiggot hole near the end. Had I been asked to appraise its value, I could not conscientiously have gone beyond fourpence.

'He's been offered five pound for that pipe,' remarked English Mrs Chi Ki, who appeared to be almost as proud of it as was her husband. 'A gentleman offered him five pound for it last autumn.'

'Why didn't he sell it, and buy another?' was my natural question; but at this old Chi Ki chuckled, and hugging the pipe chafed its bowl tenderly with his jacket cuff.

'It's worth ten pounds,' said his wife; 'it has had nothing but the best opium smoked in it these fourteen years.'

And she then went on further to enumerate the many excellences of the pipe; from which I gathered that its value was not after all so fanciful as at first appeared: since half a given quantity of opium would yield more satisfaction when smoked in a ripe, well-saturated old pipe than the whole quantity in a comparatively new one.

Chi Ki, having made all necessary preparations, got up on to the mattress on the bed, and, reclining at his ease, proceeded to load the pipe for his customer. I was curious to see how this was managed. The stuff in the gallipot looked exactly like thin treacle, and smelt like burnt sugar and laudanum. Decidedly it seemed queer stuff to load a pipe with. But it had yet to be cooked—grilled. Taking an iron bodkin from his little tool-chest, Chi Ki dipped the tip of it into the semi-liquid stuff, and withdrawing a little drop of it, held it in the flame of the lamp until it hardened somewhat. Keeping this still on the point of the bodkin, he dipped it again into the gallipot and again held it in the lamp flame, and repeated the process until a piece of the size of a large pea was accumulated and properly toasted. This was placed in the pipe-bowl, and the hungry customer sprang up on to the bed to enjoy it.

It was lit at the little lamp, and then the young Chinaman reclining at his ease, laid his head comfortably on the dirty counterpane that covered the rolled-up bed, and took the pipe-stem in his mouth. There is no mouthpiece to the pipe; the stem is cut sheer off, leaving something as thick as an office ruler to suck at. And suck the Chinaman did. He took the bamboo fairly into his mouth, and there was at once emitted from the pipe a gurgling sound—the spirits of ten thousand previously smoked pipe-loads stirred to life. As the smoker heard the delicious sound, the lids of his elongated eyes quivered in ecstasy, and he sucked harder, swallowing all the black smoke except just so little as he was bound to waste in the process of breathing. He was as economical as could be, however, and expelled but the merest thread of the precious smoke through his nostrils and none by means of his mouth. If his sensations induced by the indulgence were heavenly, his countenance grossly belied them. Gradually, as he sucked and swallowed, the veins of his forehead thickened, his cheeks flushed, and his half-closed eyes gleamed like those of a satisfied pig. Still he sucked, and the nostril wreaths came quicker and finer, and he grew more and more like an enraptured hog: when suddenly the gurgling in the throat of the pipe-stem terminated in a brief rattle, and all was over. While the opium in the pipe was waning to extremity, Chi Ki had busied himself in the manufacture of a little cigarette composed of paper and common tobacco, and as the pipe-stem dropped from the mouth of the young Chinaman, Chi Ki promptly handed him the cigarette, which he proceeded to light and consume, with a languid relish edifying to behold. I inquired why this was, but beyond the assertion that it was always done, Chi Ki had no explanation to offer.

'Was the lingering flavour of opium in the mouth objectionable?' I asked.

'No, indeed,' replied Chi Ki, with a grin; 'oh, no, no; it's always done; I don't know why, not in the least, but they will have the cigar afterwards.'

I can't help thinking, however, that this taking tobacco after opium must be something more than a meaningless 'custom'. Perhaps an abrupt and sudden descent from paradise to earth would be too much for a Chinaman's nerves, and so he applies himself to the milder narcotic by way of a gentle letting down.

From *London Society*, July 1868, author not recorded

Ten thousand scimitars flash in the sunlight

An ancient English Cathedral Tower? How can the ancient English Cathedral tower be here! The well-known massive gray square tower of its old Cathedral? How can that be here! There is no spike of rusty iron in the air, between the eye and it, from any point of the real prospect. What is the spike that intervenes, and who has set it up? Maybe it is set up by the Sultan's orders for the impaling of a horde of Turkish robbers, one by one. It is so, for cymbals clash, and the Sultan goes by to his palace in long procession. Ten thousand scimitars flash in the sunlight, and thrice ten thousand dancing-girls strew flowers. Then, follow white elephants caparisoned in countless gorgeous colours, and infinite in number and attendants. Still the Cathedral Tower rises in the background, where it cannot be, and still no writhing figure is on the grim spike. Stay! Is the spike so low a thing as the rusty spike on the top of a post of an old bedstead that has tumbled all awry? Some vague period of drowsy laughter must be devoted to the consideration of this possibility.

Shaking from head to foot, the man whose scattered consciousness has thus fantastically pieced itself together, at length rises, supports his trembling frame upon his arms, and looks around. He is in the meanest and closest of small rooms. Through the ragged window-curtain, the light of early day steals in from a miserable court. He lies, dressed, across a large unseemly bed, upon a bedstead that has indeed given way under the weight upon it. Lying, also dressed and also across the bed, not longwise, are a Chinaman, a Lascar, and a haggard woman. The two first are in a sleep or stupor; the last is blowing at a kind of pipe, to kindle it. And as she blows, and shading it with her lean hand, concentrates its red spark of light, it serves in the dim morning as a lamp to show him what he sees of her.

'Another?' says this woman, in a querulous, rattling whisper. 'Have another?'

He looks about him, with his hand to his forehead.

From *The Mystery of Edwin Drood*, 1870,
by Charles Dickens

Dorian Gray is recognised in an opium den

At the end of the room there was a little staircase, leading to a darkened chamber. As Dorian hurried up its three rickety steps, the heavy odour of opium met him. He heaved a deep breath, and his nostrils quivered with pleasure. When he entered, a young man with smooth yellow hair, who was bending over a lamp lighting a long thin pipe, looked up at him and nodded in a hesitating manner.

'You here, Adrian?' muttered Dorian.

'Where else should I be?' he answered, listlessly. 'None of the chaps will speak to me now.'

'I thought you had left England.'

'Darlington is not going to do anything. My brother paid the bill at last. George doesn't speak to me either.... I don't care,' he added with a sigh. 'As long as one has this stuff, one doesn't want friends. I think I have had too many friends.'

Dorian winced and looked round at the grotesque things that lay in such fantastic postures on the ragged mattresses. The twisted limbs, the gaping mouths, the staring lustreless eyes, fascinated him. He knew in what strange heavens they were suffering, and what dull hells were teaching them the secret of some new joy. They were better off than he was. He was prisoned in thought. Memory, like a horrible malady, was eating his soul away. From time to time he seemed to see the eyes of Basil Hallward looking at him. Yet he felt he could not stay. The presence of Adrian Singleton troubled him. He wanted to be where no one would know who he was. He wanted to escape from himself.

'I am going on to the other place,' he said after a pause.

'On the wharf?'

'Yes.'

'That mad-cat is sure to be there. They won't have her in this place now.'

Dorian shrugged his shoulders. 'I am sick of women who love one. Women who hate one are much more interesting. Besides, the stuff is better.'

'Much the same.'

'I like it better. Come and have something to drink. I must have something.'

'I don't want anything,' murmured the young man.

'Never mind.'

Adrian Singleton rose up wearily and followed Dorian to the bar. A half-caste, in a ragged turban and a shabby ulster, grinned a hideous greeting as he thrust a bottle of brandy and two tumblers in front of them. The women sidled up and began to chatter. Dorian turned his back on them and said something in a low voice to Adrian Singleton.

A crooked smile, like a Malay crease, writhed across the face of one of the women. 'We are very proud to-night,' she sneered.

'For God's sake don't talk to me,' cried Dorian, stamping his foot on the ground. 'What do you want? Money? Here it is. Don't ever talk to me again.'

Two red sparks flashed for a moment in the woman's sodden eyes, then flickered out and left them dull and glazed. She tossed her head and raked the coins off the counter with greedy fingers. Her companion watched her enviously.

'It's no use,' sighed Adrian Singleton. 'I don't care to go back. What does it matter? I am quite happy here.'

'You will write to me if you want anything, won't you?' said Dorian, after a pause.

'Perhaps.'

'Good night, then.'

'Good night,' answered the young man, passing up the steps and wiping his parched mouth with a hand-kerchief.

Dorian walked to the door with a look of pain in his face. As he drew the curtain aside, a hideous laugh broke from the painted lips of the woman who had taken his money. 'There goes the devil's bargain!' she hiccoughed, in a hoarse voice.

'Curse you!' he answered, 'don't call me that.'

She snapped her fingers. 'Prince Charming is what you like to be called, ain't it?' she yelled after him.

The drowsy sailor leaped to his feet as she spoke, and looked wildly round. The sound of the shutting of the hall door fell on his ear. He rushed out as if in pursuit.

Dorian Gray hurried along the quay through the drizzling rain. His meeting with Adrian Singleton had strangely moved him, and he wondered if the ruin of that young life was really to be laid at his door, as Basil Hallward had said to him with such infamy of insult. He bit his lip, and for a few seconds his eyes grew sad. Yet, after all, what did it matter to him? One's days were too brief to take the burden of another's errors on one's shoulders. Each man lived his own life and paid his own price for living it. The only pity was one had to pay so often for a single fault. One had to pay over and over again, indeed. In her dealings with man, destiny never closed her accounts....

Callous, concentrated on evil, with stained mind, and soul hungry for rebellion, Dorian Gray hastened on, quickening his step as he went, but as he darted aside into a dim archway, that had served him often as a short cut to the ill-famed place where he was going, he felt himself suddenly seized from behind, and before he had time to defend himself, he was thrust back against the wall, with a brutal hand round his throat.

He struggled madly for life, and by a terrible effort wrenched the tightening fingers away. In a second he heard the click of a revolver, and saw the gleam of a polished barrel, pointing straight at his head, and the dusky form of a short, thick-set man facing him.

'What do you want?' he gasped.

'Keep quiet,' said the man. 'If you stir, I shoot you.'

'You are mad. What have I done to you?'

'You wrecked the life of Sibyl Vane,' was the answer,

'and Sibyl Vane was my sister. She killed herself. I know it. Her death is at your door. I swore I would kill you in return. For years I have sought you. I had no clue, no trace. The two people who could have described you were dead. I knew nothing of you but the pet name she used to call you. I heard it to-night by chance. Make your peace with God, for to-night you are going to die.'

Dorian Gray grew sick with fear. 'I never knew her,' he stammered. 'I never heard of her. You are mad.'

'You had better confess your sin, for as sure as I am James Vane, you are going to die.' There was a horrible moment. Dorian did not know what to say or do. 'Down on your knees!' growled the man. 'I give you one minute to make your peace—no more. I go on board to-night for India, and I must do my job first. One minute. That's all.'

Dorian's arms fell to his side. Paralysed with terror, he did not know what to do. Suddenly a wild hope flashed across his brain. 'Stop,' he cried. 'How long ago is it since your sister died? Quick, tell me!'

'Eighteen years,' said the man. 'Why do you ask me? What do years matter?'

'Eighteen years,' laughed Dorian Gray, with a touch of triumph in his voice. 'Eighteen years! Set me under the lamp and look at my face!'

James Vane hesitated for a moment, not understanding what was meant. Then he seized Dorian

Gray and dragged him from the archway.

Dim and wavering as was the wind-blown light, yet it served to show him the hideous error, as it seemed, into which he had fallen, for the face of the man he had sought to kill had all the bloom of boyhood, all the unstained purity of youth. He seemed little more than a lad of twenty summers, hardly older, if older indeed at all, than his sister had been when they had parted so many years ago. It was obvious that this was not the man who had destroyed her life.

He loosened his hold and reeled back. 'My God! my God!' he cried, 'and I would have murdered you!'

Dorian Gray drew a long breath. 'You have been on the brink of committing a terrible crime, my man,' he said, looking at him sternly. 'Let this be a warning to you not to take vengeance into your own hands.'

'Forgive me, sir,' muttered James Vane. 'I was deceived. A chance word I heard in that damned den set me on the wrong track.'

'You had better go home and put that pistol away, or you may get into trouble,' said Dorian, turning on his heel and going slowly down the street.

From *The Picture of Dorian Gray*, 1891,
by Oscar Wilde

A doddering, loose-lipped senility

I walked down the narrow passage between the double row of sleepers, holding my breath to keep out

the vile, stupefying fumes of the drug, and looking
about for the manager. As I passed the tall man who
sat by the brazier I felt a sudden pluck at my skirt,
and a low voice whispered, 'Walk past me, and then
look back at me.' The words fell quite distinctly upon
my ear. I glanced down. They could only have come
from the old man at my side, and yet he sat now as
absorbed as ever, very thin, very wrinkled, bent with
age, an opium pipe dangling down from between
his knees, as though it had dropped in sheer lassi-
tude from his fingers. I took two steps forward and
looked back. It took all my self-control to prevent me
from breaking out into a cry of astonishment. He had
turned his back so that none could see him but I. His
form had filled out, his wrinkles were gone, the dull
eyes had regained their fire, and there, sitting by the
fire and grinning at my surprise, was none other than
Sherlock Holmes.

He made a slight motion to me to approach him,
and instantly, as he turned his face half round to the
company once more, subsided into a doddering,
loose-lipped senility.

From *The Man with the Twisted Lip*
by Sir Arthur Conan Doyle, 1891

WAR

The chapter begins with a poem by E. Nesbit. Edith Nesbit (1858–1924) was an English author and poet whose children's works were published under the name of E. Nesbit. Her best-known work is, perhaps, *The Railway Children*. Gore Vidal praised the sophistication of her work, comparing her favourably with another great English writer: 'After Lewis Carroll, E. Nesbit is the best of the English fabulists who wrote about children (neither wrote *for* children) and like Carroll she was able to create a world of magic and inverted logic that was entirely her own.' She wrote a sequence of war poems that have been unjustly yet understandably neglected, eclipsed by the work of combatants such as Sassoon and Owen.

Anthony Powell (1905–2000) saw military service as an infantry subaltern in Ulster and as a military liaison officer in the intelligence corps, attached to a series of governments in exile. These experiences shaped the war passages in his twelve-volume sequence of novels, *A Dance to the Music of Time*. What Powell captures very neatly, a quality that is consistently admired by serving military personnel who read his works, is the inertia of war and the boredom that this engenders. Even the now famous 'silence' before the eventual strike of a flying bomb is secondary to the diversions that the narrator, Nick Jenkins, and his NCO are obliged to devise in order to keep themselves awake while on Fire Duty.

There is a similarly inward-looking passage, reproduced here, in *The War of the Worlds* by H.G. Wells (1866–1946). Here, the narrator and a stray artilleryman get quietly drunk whilst playing cards, using areas of London as imaginary 'chips'. Beneath them, London lies in ruins and panic in the wake of the Martian invaders.

The passage from Saki's unsettling novel *When William Came* describes what Piccadilly might have been like in the event that Britain allowed the Germans in rather than going to war with them. Saki was the pseudonym of H.H. Munro (1870–1916), who is chiefly remembered for his darkly humorous short stories featuring the young men Clovis and Reginald and the various aunts, dowagers and social climbers in their circle. But behind all this, Munro was an unbending patriot and the intention behind *When William Came* was to expose what he saw as an increasingly spineless mentality in Edwardian Britain. His concerns proved groundless, but the novel constitutes an interesting essay on what it means to 'give up' out of expediency rather than fight to the bitter end.

E. Nesbit: *In Hospital* (1916)

Under the shadow of a hawthorn brake,
Where bluebells draw the sky down to the wood,
Where, 'mid brown leaves, the primroses awake
And hidden violets smell of solitude;
Beneath green leaves bright-fluttered by the wing
Of fleeting, beautiful, immortal Spring,
I should have said, 'I love you,' and your eyes
Have said, 'I, too...' The gods saw otherwise.

For this is winter, and the London streets
Are full of soldiers from that far, fierce fray
Where life knows death, and where poor glory meets
Full-face with shame, and weeps and turns away.
And in the broken, trampled foreign wood
Is horror, and the terrible scent of blood,
And love shines tremulous, like a drowning star,
Under the shadow of the wings of war.

Anthony Powell on Fire Duty

Fire Duty was something that came round at regular intervals. It meant hanging about the building all night, fully dressed, prepared to go on the roof, if the Warning sounded, with the object of extinguishing incendiary bombs that might fall there. These were said to be easily dealt with by use of sand and an instrument like a garden hoe, both of which were provided as equipment. On previous occasions, up to now, no raid had occurred, the hours passing not too unpleasantly with a book. Feeling I needed a change from the seventeenth century and Proust, I had brought Saltykov-Schredin's *The Golovlyov Family* to read. A more trivial choice would have been humiliating, because Corporal Curtis turned out to be the accompanying NCO that night, and had *Adam Bede* under his arm. We made whatever mutual arrangements were required, then retired to our respective off-duty locations.

Towards midnight I was examining a collection of photographs taken on D-Day, which had not long before this replaced the two Isbister-like oil paintings. Why the pictures had been removed after being allowed to hang throughout the earlier years of the blitz was not apparent. Mime, now a captain, had just hurried past with his telegrams, when the Warning sounded. I found my way to the roof at the same moment as Corporal Curtis.

'I understand, sir, that we ascend into one of the cupolas as an action station.'

'We do.'

'I thought I had better await your arrival and instructions, sir.'

'Tell me the plot of *Adam Bede* as far as you've got. I've never read it.'

Like the muezzin going on duty, we climbed up a steep gangway of iron leading into one of the pepper-pot domes constructed at each corner of the building. The particular dome allotted to us, the one nearest the river, was on the far side from that above our own room. The inside was on two floors, rather like an eccentric writer's den for undisturbed work. Curtis and I proceeded to the upper level. These Edwardian belvederes, elaborately pillared and corniced like Temples of Love in a rococo garden, were not in themselves of exceptional beauty, and, when first erected, must have seemed obscure in functional purpose. Now, however, the architect's design showed prophetic aptitude. The exigencies of war had transformed them into true gazebos, not, as it turned out, frequented to observe the pleasing prospects with which such rotundas and follies were commonly associated, but at least to view their antithesis, 'horridly gothick' aspects of the heavens, lit up by fire and rent with thunder.

This extension of purpose was given effect a minute or two later. The moonlit night, now the melancholy strain of the sirens had died away, was surprisingly quiet. All Ack-Ack guns had been sent to the coast, for there was no point in shooting down V1s over built-up areas. They would come down anyway. Around lay the darkened city, a few solid masses, like the Donners-Brebner Building, recognizable on the far side of the twisting strip of water. Then three rapidly moving lights appeared in the southern sky, two more or less side by side, the third following a short way behind, as if lacking acceleration or will power to keep up. They travelled with that curious shuddering jerky movement characteristic of such bodies, a style of locomotion that seemed to suggest the engine was not working properly, might break down at any moment, which indeed it would. This impression that something was badly wrong with the internal machinery was increased by a shower of sparks emitted from the tail. A more exciting possibility was that dragons were flying through the air in a fabulous tale, and climbing into the turret with Curtis had been done in a dream. The raucous buzz could now be plainly heard. In imagination one smelt brimstone.

'They appear to be heading a few degrees to our right, sir,' said Curtis.

The first two cut-out. It was almost simultaneous. The noisy ticking of the third continued briefly, then also stopped abruptly This interval between cutting-out and exploding always seemed interminable. At last it came; again two almost at once, the third a few seconds later. All three swooped to the ground, their flaming tails pointing upwards, certainly dragons now, darting earthward to consume their prey of maidens chained to rocks.

'Southwark, do you think?'

'Lambeth, sir—having regard to the incurvations of the river.'

'Sweet Thames run softly ...'

'I was thinking the same, sir.'

'I'm afraid they've caught it, whichever it was.'

'I'm afraid so, sir.'

The All Clear sounded. We climbed down the iron gangway. 'Do you think that will be all for tonight?'

'I hope so, sir. Just to carry the story on from where we were when we were interrupted: Hetty is then convicted of the murder of her child and transported.'

From *The Military Philosophers*, 1968

H.G. Wells on the Martians in London

From this position a shrubbery hid the greater portion of Putney, but we could see the river below, a bubbly mass of red weed, and the low parts of Lambeth flooded and red. The red creeper swarmed up the trees about the old palace, and their branches stretched gaunt and dead, and set with shrivelled leaves, from amid its clusters. It was strange how entirely dependent both these things were upon flowing water for their propagation. About us neither had gained a footing; laburnums, pink mays, snowballs, and trees of arbor-vitae, rose out of laurels and hydrangeas, green and brilliant into the sunlight. Beyond Kensington dense smoke was rising, and that and a blue haze hid the northward hills.

The artilleryman began to tell me of the sort of people who still remained in London.

'One night last week,' he said, 'some fools got the electric light in order, and there was all Regent Street and the Circus ablaze, crowded with painted and ragged drunkards, men and women, dancing and shouting till dawn. A man who was there told me. And as the day came they became aware of a fighting-machine standing near by the Langham and looking down at them. Heaven knows how long he had been there. It must have given some of them a nasty turn. He came down the road towards them, and picked up nearly a hundred too drunk or frightened to run away.'

Grotesque gleam of a time no history will ever fully describe!

From that, in answer to my questions, he came round to his grandiose plans again. He grew enthusiastic. He talked so eloquently of the possibility of capturing a fighting-machine that I more than half believed in him again. But now that I was beginning to understand something of his quality, I could divine the stress he laid on doing nothing precipitately. And I noted that now there was no question that he personally was to capture and fight the great machine.

After a time we went down to the cellar. Neither of us seemed disposed to resume digging, and when he suggested a meal, I was nothing loath. He became suddenly very generous, and when we had eaten he went away and returned with some excellent cigars.

We lit these, and his optimism glowed. He was inclined to regard my coming as a great occasion.

'There's some champagne in the cellar,' he said.

'We can dig better on this Thames-side burgundy,' said I.

'No,' said he; 'I am host today. Champagne! Great God! We've a heavy enough task before us! Let us take a rest and gather strength while we may. Look at these blistered hands!'

And pursuant to this idea of a holiday, he insisted upon playing cards after we had eaten. He taught me euchre, and after dividing London between us, I taking the northern side and he the southern, we played for parish points. Grotesque and foolish as this will seem to the sober reader, it is absolutely true, and what is more remarkable, I found the card game and several others we played extremely interesting.

Strange mind of man! that, with our species upon the edge of extermination or appalling degradation, with no clear prospect before us but the chance of a horrible death, we could sit following the chance of this painted pasteboard, and playing the 'joker' with vivid delight. Afterwards he taught me poker, and I beat him at three tough chess games. When dark came we decided to take the risk, and lit a lamp.

After an interminable string of games, we supped, and the artilleryman finished the champagne. We went on smoking the cigars. He was no longer the energetic regenerator of his species I had encountered in the morning. He was still optimistic, but it was a less kinetic, a more thoughtful optimism. I remember he wound up with my health, proposed in a speech of small variety and considerable intermittence. I took a cigar, and went upstairs to look at the lights of which he had spoken that blazed so greenly along the Highgate hills.

At first I stared unintelligently across the London valley. The northern hills were shrouded in darkness; the fires near Kensington glowed redly, and now and then an orange-red tongue of flame flashed up and vanished in the deep blue night. All the rest of London was black. Then, nearer, I perceived a strange light, a pale, violet-purple fluorescent glow, quivering under the night breeze. For a space I could not understand it, and then I knew that it must be the red weed from which this faint irradiation proceeded. With that realisation my dormant sense of wonder, my sense of the proportion of things, awoke again. I glanced from that to Mars, red and clear, glowing high in the west, and then gazed long and earnestly at the darkness of Hampstead and Highgate.

I remained a very long time upon the roof, wondering at the grotesque changes of the day. I recalled my mental states from the midnight prayer to the foolish card-playing. I had a violent revulsion of feeling. I remember I flung away the cigar with a certain waste-

ful symbolism. My folly came to me with glaring exaggeration. I seemed a traitor to my wife and to my
kind; I was filled with remorse. I resolved to leave this
strange undisciplined dreamer of great things to his
drink and gluttony, and to go on into London. There,
it seemed to me, I had the best chance of learning
what the Martians and my fellow men were doing. I
was still upon the roof when the late moon rose.

From *The War of the Worlds*, 1898

Saki on an occupied London

The Green Park end of Piccadilly was a changed, and
in some respects a livelier thoroughfare to that which
Yeovil remembered with affectionate regret. A great
political club had migrated from its palatial home to
a shrunken habitation in a less prosperous quarter;
its place was filled by the flamboyant frontage of the
Hotel Konstantinopel. Gorgeous Turkey carpets were
spread over the wide entrance steps, and boys in
Circassian and Anatolian costumes hung around the
doors, or dashed forth in un-Oriental haste to carry
such messages as the telephone was unable to trans-
mit. Picturesque sellers of Turkish delight, attar-of-
roses, and brass-work coffee services, squatted under
the portico, on terms of obvious good understanding with the hotel management. A few doors further
down a service club that had long been a Piccadilly
landmark was a landmark still, as the home of the

Army Aeronaut Club, and there was a constant coming and going of gay-hued uniforms, Saxon, Prussian, Bavarian, Hessian, and so forth, through its portals. The mastering of the air and the creation of a scientific aerial war fleet, second to none in the world, was an achievement of which the conquering race was pardonably proud, and for which it had good reason to be duly thankful. Over the gateways was blazoned the badge of the club, an elephant, whale, and eagle, typifying the three armed forces of the State, by land and sea and air; the eagle bore in its beak a scroll with the proud legend: 'The last am I, but not the least.'

To the eastward of this gaily-humming hive the long shuttered front of a deserted ducal mansion struck a note of protest and mourning amid the noise and whirl and colour of a seemingly uncaring city. On the other side of the roadway, on the gravelled paths of the Green Park, small ragged children from the back streets of Westminster looked wistfully at the smooth trim stretches of grass on which it was now forbidden, in two languages, to set foot. Only the pigeons, disregarding the changes of political geography, walked about as usual, wondering perhaps, if they ever wondered at anything, at the sudden change in the distribution of park humans.

Yeovil turned his steps out of the hot sunlight into the shade of the Burlington Arcade, familiarly known to many of its newer frequenters as the Passage. Here

the change that new conditions and requirements
had wrought was more immediately noticeable than
anywhere else in the West End. Most of the shops on
the western side had been cleared away, and in their
place had been installed an 'open-air' café, converting
the long alley into a sort of promenade tea-garden,
flanked on one side by a line of haberdashers', per-
fumers', and jewellers' show windows. The patrons
of the café could sit at the little round tables, drinking their coffee and syrups and apéritifs, and gazing,
if they were so minded, at the pyjamas and cravats
and Brazilian diamonds spread out for inspection
before them. A string orchestra, hidden away somewhere in a gallery, was alternating grand opera with
the *Gondola Girl* and the latest gems of Transatlantic
melody. From around the tightly-packed tables arose
a babble of tongues, made up chiefly of German, a
South American rendering of Spanish, and a North
American rendering of English, with here and there
the sharp shaken-out staccato of Japanese. A sleepy-
looking boy, in a nondescript uniform, was wandering to and fro among the customers, offering for sale
the *Matin*, *New York Herald*, *Berliner Tageblatt*, and a
host of crudely coloured illustrated papers, embody-
ing the hard-worked wit of a world-legion of comic
artists. Yeovil hurried through the Arcade; it was not
here, in this atmosphere of staring alien eyes and jan-
gling tongues, that he wanted to read the news of the

Imperial *Aufklärung*.

By a succession of by-ways he reached Hanover Square, and thence made his way into Oxford Street. There was no commotion of activity to be noticed yet among the newsboys; the posters still concerned themselves with the earthquake in Hungary, varied with references to the health of the King of Roumania, and a motor accident in South London. Yeovil wandered aimlessly along the street for a few dozen yards, and then turned down into the smoking-room of a cheap tea-shop, where he judged that the flourishing foreign element would be less conspicuously represented. Quiet-voiced, smooth-headed youths, from neighbouring shops and wholesale houses, sat drinking tea and munching pastry, some of them reading, others making a fitful rattle with dominoes on the marble-topped tables. A clean, wholesome smell of tea and coffee made itself felt through the clouds of cigarette smoke; cleanliness and listlessness seemed to be the dominant notes of the place, a cleanliness that was commendable, and a listlessness that seemed unnatural and undesirable where so much youth was gathered together for refreshment and recreation. Yeovil seated himself at a table already occupied by a young clergyman who was smoking a cigarette over the remains of a plateful of buttered toast. He had a keen, clever, hard-lined face, the face of a man who, in an earlier stage of European history, might have been a warlike prior, awkward to tackle at the council-board, greatly to be avoided where blows were being exchanged. A pale, silent damsel drifted up to Yeovil and took his order with an air of being mentally some hundreds of miles away, and utterly indifferent to the requirements of those whom she served; if she had brought calf's-foot jelly instead of the pot of China tea he had asked for, Yeovil would hardly have been surprised. However, the tea duly arrived on the table, and the pale damsel scribbled a figure on a slip of paper, put it silently by the side of the teapot, and drifted silently away. Yeovil had seen the same sort of thing done on the musical-comedy stage, and done rather differently.

'Can you tell me, sir, is the Imperial announcement out yet?' asked the young clergyman, after a brief scrutiny of his neighbour.

From *When William Came*, 1913

LIONS & TIGERS
CATS & DOGS

There have always been animals in London, both domestic and wild, from the exotic creatures kept in me-
nageries to pampered pooches kept for companionship.
Alongside these are the strays, many of them impound-
ed in the famous dogs' home at Battersea.

The tradition of holding wild animals captive in the
capital began in the Middle Ages and continues to the
present day. Many of the early animals were gifts from
foreign ambassadors. For centuries they were kept in
the menagerie at the Tower of London and remained
a popular attraction. One of the first and most striking was the polar bear acquired from Norway in the
13th century. Several monarchs took a keen interest in
the menagerie, including James I, who in 1603 built a
viewing gallery at the lions' enclosure and a trough 'for
the Lyons to drinke and wasche themselves in'. Many
exotic creatures came and went but the lions remained
the principal attraction, possibly because there were so
many of them, the lion being an emblem of England
and as such a perfect ambassadorial gift. Throughout
the 17th century the lion cubs were allowed to roam
freely within the precincts of the Tower, much to the
delight of younger visitors. As one would expect, all the

animals had names. Pepys recalls 'Crowly, who is now grown a very great lion and very tame'; the Tower guide book of 1741 mentions the lions Marco and Phillis and their son Nero along with Dicka the tiger cub and Willa the leopard; then there was Old Martin, a grizzly bear said to be nearly 100 years old in 1823, deeply unsociable, who treated his keepers as 'perfect strangers' even after decades of captivity. The 18th century saw the inauguration of a 'School of Monkeys', presided over by an ill-tempered and unpredictable baboon who would 'heave anything that happens to be within his reach with such Force as to split Stools, Bowls and other Wooden Utensils in a Hundred Pieces'. Visitors were warned that a young baboon is 'gay, playful and docile', 'but as he grows older he becomes intractable, malicious and ferocious'. The elephants were said to be 'fond of wine, spirits and other intoxicating articles' and were allowed a gallon of wine a day. When it closed in 1835, the Tower menagerie had upwards of 280 animals, many of whom were moved to the newly-built London Zoo in Regent's Park where they formed the foundation of the new collection.

Thomas Pennant (1726–98) and Richard Phillips (1767–1840) both give accounts of the Tower menagerie. Pennant was a naturalist, traveller and writer whose *British Zoology* was highly respected in its day. Phillips was a teacher, author and publisher who wrote interesting accounts of London life. He mentions 'Tippoo Sahib', referring to Tipu Sultan, a Mughal prince known as the 'Tiger of Mysore', an implacable enemy of the British, who was killed at the fall of Srirangapattana in 1799. There is, in the Victoria & Albert Museum, a large mechanical tiger commissioned by Tipu. When a handle was turned (in the interests of conservation, it no longer is), the tiger 'mauls' a recumbent British soldier and a clever mechanism imitates the tiger's growls and the groans of the victim.

Pierce Egan (*see p. 36*) relates Dr Johnson's encounter with a bear at Southwark, a popular pleasure resort in those days with a great many sideshows on offer.

There are two 19th-century accounts of London Zoo, by Mrs Jane Ellen Panton (1847–1923) and by the maverick priest Augustus Stopford Brooke (1832–1916), both of which provoke a sense of unease at the plight of animals in captivity. Mrs Panton, the daughter of the artist William Powell Frith, had many London literary friends including Wilkie Collins, of whom she tells an amusing story worth quoting in full: 'I think the most embarrassing evening I ever spent at the play was when I accompanied Wilkie Collins to see a three-act mystery which he and Charles Reade had concocted together [*Rank and Riches* (1883)]. Both were in the most intense state of nervousness, Wilkie sitting behind the curtain biting his nails, and Charles Reade was in and out of the box constantly, using the strongest of strong language and driving me nearly wild. The whole play turned on the finding of some document which had been hidden behind a brick in a bed-room wall, a most obvious brick, plainly to be seen by the least observant person. The detectives came in and tapped in every place save the right one, until the gallery could bear it no longer and called out which the brick was. That damned the play; all the fine sentiments of the hero were screamed at, and howls and cat-calls finally brought down the curtain, while Wilkie Collins and Charles Reade fiercely condemned the British public to eternal damnation, and we went home delighted to get away from the company of the unhappy authors.'

Turning to fiction, it is easy to forget, in the wake of so many 'Gothic' film adaptations, that Bram Stoker's *Dracula* contains some comic episodes. One of the finest, reproduced here, relates the antics of Bersicker, the wolf at London Zoo. The 'Jamrach's' alluded to was a real-life enterprise, a travelling zoo run by the entrepreneur Charles Jamrach (1815–91), whose stirring account of an escaped tiger, written for the *Boy's Own* paper, is reproduced here.

The English have always been famously sentimental about their pets. At the time of writing a £4000 reward has been paid for the safe return of a dog lost in Hampstead, North West London. Pets are as popular in London as they ever were although the 'lost' notices put up today are by no means as elegantly crafted as the one reproduced here. Nor is there today a dog-kidnapping racket as widespread and well-organised as that described by Henry Mayhew. Lost dogs, if they did not end up as bargaining chips for ransom, would in the late 19th century have been rounded up and sent to Battersea Dogs' Home. Founded in 1860 by Mrs Mary Tealby, the Dogs' Home was first known as the 'Temporary Home for Lost and Starving Dogs'. There is—or was—also a causal link between the welfare of the animals in the Tower and the disappearance of domestic pets: in the 1720s it cost threepence to see the lions, a fee that had risen to ninepence by the end of the century; however, free entry was granted to anyone who brought a dead dog or cat to supplement the lions' and tiger's daily diet of raw beef.

Dr Johnson praises his cat Hodge, for whom he bought oysters. His gruff but intense affection for this cat is well known: when Hodge was dying, Johnson brought valerian to ease the pain of the last hours, a small, perfectly considered and highly characteristic act of kindness.

Finally, there are those other 'animals', human beings incarcerated because of their inability to function in normal society, and exposed to the merriment of others, as shown by the extract on the infamous Bethlehem Royal Hospital in Beckenham, known as Bedlam, an institution for the insane. The practice of publicly exhibiting the mental patients and charging an admission fee was hugely popular until it was banned in 1770.

Six pence a day, for the sustenance of the leopards

Edward IV built the Lions tower: it was originally
called Bulwark; but received the former name from
its use. A menagery had very long been a piece of re-
gal state. Henry I had his at his manor of Woodstock,
where he kept lions, leopards, lynxes, porcupines,
and several other uncommon beasts. They were
afterwards removed to the Tower. Edward II commanded the sheriffs of London to pay the keepers of
the king's leopards six pence a day, for the sustenance
of the leopards; and three half-pence a day for the
diet of the keeper, out of the fee-farm of the city. I
should have mentioned before, that Henry issued his
order to the sheriffs, to supply four pence a day for
the maintenance of his white bear (*urso nostro albo*),
and his keeper, in the Tower of London. They were
also to provide a muzzle, and an iron chain to hold
the said bear out of the water; and a long cord to
hold it during the time it was fishing in the Thames:
they were besides ordered to build a small house in
the Tower for the king's elephant (*elefantem nostrum*)
and to make provision both for beast and keeper.
The royal menagery is to this day exceedingly well
supplied. In April 1787, there was a leopard, of a
quite unknown species, brought from Bengal. It was
wholly black, but the hair was marked, on the back,
sides, and neck, with round clutters of small spots,
of a glossy and the most intense black; the tail hung

several inches beyond the length of the legs, and was very full of hair. Here were also two tigers: one had been here some time, and its ground-colour had faded into a pale sickly sandiness; the other, young and vigorous, and almost fresh from its native woods, was almost of an orange colour; and its black stripes, and the white parts, were most pure in their kinds.

From Thomas Pennant's *Of London*, 1790

The Tower Menagerie

[The animals are] kept in a yard at the west entrance. A figure of a lion is over the door, and there is a bell at the side to call the keeper. The visitor pays a shilling here, for which the keeper shows him all the wild beasts, explaining their several histories. The principal of these at present in the Tower consist of lions, tigers, leopards, panthers, the laughing hyenas, the Spanish wolf, the ant-bear, and some mountain cats and racoons. Among them are, or latterly were, three royal hunting tigers, which are said to have belonged to a pack of the same kind kept by Tippoo Sahib, with which he hunted beasts of prey. That part of the menagerie over which is the terrace of which we have spoken above was formerly called the house of the 'great carnivora'. Here were exhibited, in dens, the lions, tigers, leopards, jaguars, panthers &c; but at the commencement of 1786 they were removed to more spacious and comfortable quarters in a new 'lion house', which is situated a little further to the south, not far from the ponds set apart for the seals and sealions. The noble beasts made the journey, not in a sort of quiet and sober procession, and as they are seen in pictures of Bacchus and his attendant train, but in closed boxes, with slipped sides, into which they were tempted by the sight of some extra slices of meat. This done, they were transported on trucks, in a most unroyal and ignoble manner, to the new abode, where the closed box was placed against the front bars of the new den, into which they were only too glad to make their way. The new 'lion house' is excellently constructed and well warmed; and far more persons are now able to watch its inmates dine at four o'clock on Sunday afternoons in 'the season' than was the case before this change was made.

From *Modern London*, 1804, by Richard Phillips

Dr Johnson meets a bear

When the Doctor first became acquainted with David Mallet, they once went, with some other gentlemen, to laugh away an hour at Southwark-fair. At one of the booths where wild beasts were exhibited to the wondering crowd, was a very large bear, which the showman assured them was 'cotched' in the undiscovered deserts of the remotest Russia. The bear was muzzled, and might therefore be approached with safety; but to all the company, except Johnson, was very surly and ill tempered. Of the philosopher he appeared extremely fond, rubbed against him, and displayed every mark of awkward partiality, and ursine kindness. 'How is it,' (said one of the company) 'that this savage animal is so attached to Mr Johnson?' 'From a very natural cause, replied Mallet: the bear is a Russian philosopher, and he knows that Linnæus would have placed him in the same class with the English moralist. They are two barbarous animals of one species.' Johnson disliked Mallet for his tendency to infidelity, and this sarcasm turned his dislike into downright hatred. He never spoke to him afterwards, but has gibbeted him in his octavo dictionary, under the article 'Alias'.

From Pierce Egan's *Life in London*, 1821

Mrs Panton on memories of London Zoo

[I] well recollect how dismally [I] suffered from the agonised howls from the Zoological Gardens on Sundays, and I think these first gave me the religious doubts I have always possessed. From my earliest days I have adored animals. I would cause Miss D— anguish by patting every stray dog we met in our walks, and by catching up and kissing every dirty little kitten, and the animals in the Gardens were very near and dear to my heart. Would it be believed that in those days the wretched creatures were not fed from Saturday night until Monday morning, by which time the neighbourhood resounded with their savage howls? The noise I believe, and not the animals' sufferings, was the cause of this wicked cruelty being knocked on the head, and I can well remember saving, aye and stealing, bits to give to the creatures, when we used to go to see them on Sunday afternoons. We were always at the Zoological Gardens; we not only had friends who gave us the green tickets, but we knew the keepers, one of whom lived in a lodge where we sometimes had tea, which always smelt of lion, and which now and then contained baby lions or other beasts, very small, very soft; which were being warmed and fed in front of his fire, and which I distinctly remember being allowed to nurse. I further recollect the feel of the rough tongues which licked our fingers, and being solemnly warned not to allow them to draw blood, for we were given to understand that, if they once tasted blood, the soft little kitteny things would become violent and gobble us up on the spot. Once I was in very real peril in these same gardens; I did not know that the horrible creature advancing towards me dragging a bit of chain and waving a stick was an escaped ourang-outang—the one specimen, I believe, then in any civilised country—and I was about to try and make friends when a white-faced keeper, followed by two or three other men, sprang out of the bushes and seized the chain; afterwards I heard the nurse tell my mother of the dreadful risk I had run, for our keeper friend had told her if they had not caught the beast when they did, he would have torn me limb from limb. I can't say if he would; I saw an ourang-outang the other day which did not look so very large or so very alarming, yet I distinctly remember the beast towering above me, so I think I must have been quite small enough to demolish if he had desired to do so. Yet another monkey obtained my undying hatred by stretching out a long lean arm, and grabbing a beautiful long feather out of my best hat, and when I stamped and raved with rage the beast ran up to the top of the cage, and tore it into the smallest of atoms...

But much as I loved the gardens then, I love them a thousand times more now, when the animals are decently housed and treated, called by their names and looked after by their keepers, who really understand and care for their charges. The only thing that remains to be done is to teach the public to behave, to cease to prod the beasts with 'swagger sticks', and to realise that monkeys don't eat sardine-tin lids or orange peel; and that the beautiful tame squirrels that now run fearlessly about the place, will soon lose their confidence in humanity if they are teased as they are at present, and not made friends with as they are in the Central Park in New York.

From *Leaves from a Life*, 1908

Augustus Stopford Brooke visits London Zoo

May 30, 1899:—Went to the Zoo with Arthur. All the beasts were asleep when we arrived except a bear or two. The Polar Bear was like one of our decadent poets, marching up and down in his own poems. The two Grizzly Bears are young and innocent, I think, of blood. The old grayheaded villain who used to be here, and who was blind, is dead. He had slain his foes. I always saw his claws ruddy with gore. All the lions, tigers, etc., were munching bones, like American capitalists. A new giraffe has come, a young, guileless male; a lily, a birch-sapling, destined to be husband when he reaches puberty, of a huge female, huge in comparison with this boy, who looks at him now over a high wooden ledge with infinite scorn. The Rhinoceroses were sound asleep, pillowed on hay, and one had covered his eyes with straw. They snored, and shook the house. The Hippo has got huge warts on his hind feet, and hates them. If ever I saw a weary cynic, I saw the creature in him. Walked home through the park, a warm, dull, gray, vicious day! No colour anywhere.

From the *Diary*, 1899

Count Dracula visits London Zoo

'All right, guv'nor. This 'ere is about the 'ole story. That 'ere wolf what we called Bersicker was one of three gray ones that came from Norway to Jamrach's, which we bought off him four years ago. He was a nice well-behaved wolf, that never gave no trouble to talk of. I'm more surprised at 'im for wantin' to get out nor any other animile in the place. But, there, you can't trust wolves no more nor women.'

'Don't you mind him, Sir!' broke in Mrs Tom, with a cheery laugh. ''E's got mindin' the animiles so long that blest if he ain't like a old wolf 'isself! But there ain't no 'arm in 'im.'

'Well, Sir, it was about two hours after feedin' yesterday when I first hear my disturbance. I was makin' up a litter in the monkey house for a young puma which is ill. But when I heard the yelpin' and 'owlin' I kem away straight. There was Bersicker a-tearin' like a mad thing at the bars as if he wanted to get out. There wasn't much people about that day, and close at hand was only one man, a tall, thin chap, with a 'ook nose and a pointed beard, with a few white hairs runnin' through it. He had a 'ard, cold look and red eyes, and I took a sort of mislike to him, for it seemed as if it was 'im as they was hirritated at. He 'ad white kid gloves on 'is 'ands, and he pointed out the animiles to me and says, "Keeper, these wolves seem upset at something."

"Maybe it's you," says I, for I did not like the airs as he give 'isself. He didn't get angry, as I 'oped he would, but he smiled a kind of insolent smile, with a mouth full of white, sharp teeth. "Oh no, they wouldn't like me," 'e says.

"Ow yes, they would," says I, a-imitatin' of him. "They always like a bone or two to clean their teeth on about tea time, which you 'as a bagful."

Well, it was a odd thing, but when the animiles see us a-talkin' they lay down, and when I went over to Bersicker he let me stroke his ears same as ever. That there man kem over, and blessed but if he didn't put in his hand and stroke the old wolf's ears too!

"Tyke care," says I. "Bersicker is quick."

"Never mind," he says, "I'm used to 'em!"

"Are you in the business yourself?" I says, tyking off my 'at, for a man what trades in wolves, anceterer, is a good friend to keepers.

"No," says he, "not exactly in the business, but I 'ave made pets of several." And with that he lifts his 'at as perlite as a lord, and walks away.'

From *Dracula* by Bram Stoker, 1897

Charles Jamrach struggles with a tiger

It is now a good many years ago, when one morning a van-load of wild beasts, which I had bought the previous day from a captain in the London Docks, who brought them from the East Indies, arrived at my repository in Betts Street, St George's in-the-East. I myself superintended the unloading of the animals, and had given directions to my men to place a den containing a very ferocious full-grown Bengal tiger, with its iron-barred front close against the wall.

They were proceeding to take down a den with leopards, when all of a sudden I heard a crash, and to my horror found the big tiger had pushed out the back part of his den with his hind-quarters, and was walking down the yard into the street, which was then full of people watching the arrival of this curious merchandise. The tiger, in putting his forepaws against the iron bars in front of the den, had exerted his full strength to push with his back against the boards behind, and had thus succeeded in gaining his liberty. As soon as he got into the street, a boy of about nine years of age put out his hand to stroke the beast's back, when the tiger seized him by the shoulder and run down the street with the lad hanging in his jaws. This was done in less time than it takes me to relate; but when I saw the boy being carried off in this manner, and witnessed the panic that had seized hold of the people, without further thought I dashed after the brute, and got hold of him by the loose skin of the back of his neck. I was then of a more vigorous frame than now, and had plenty of pluck and dash in me.

I tried thus to stop his further progress, but he was too strong for me, and dragged me, too, along with him. I then succeeded in putting my leg under his hind legs, tripping him up, so to say, and he fell in consequence on his knees. I now, with all my strength and weight, knelt on him, and releasing the loose skin I had hold of, I pushed my thumbs with all my strength behind his ears, trying to strangulate him thus. All this time the beast held fast to the boy.

My men had been seized with the same panic as the bystanders, but now I discovered one lurking round a corner, so I shouted to him to come with a crowbar; he fetched one, and hit the tiger three tremendous blows over the eyes.

It was only now he released the boy. His jaws opened and his tongue protruded about seven inches. I thought the brute was dead or dying, and let go of him, but no sooner had I done so than he jumped up again. In the same moment I seized the crowbar myself, and gave him, with all the strength I had left, a blow over his head. He seemed to be quite cowed, and, turning tail, went back towards the stables, which fortunately were open. I drove him into the yard, and closed the doors at once. Looking round for my tiger, I found he had sneaked into a large empty den that stood open at the bottom of the yard. Two of my men, who had jumped on to an elephant's box, now descended, and pushed down the iron-barred sliding-door of the den; and so my tiger was safe again under lock and key.

The boy was taken to the hospital, but with the exception of a fright and a scratch, was very little hurt. I lost no time in making inquiry about him, and finding where his father was, I offered him £50 as some compensation for the alarm he had sustained. Nevertheless, the father, a tailor, brought an action against me for damages, and I had to pay £300, of which he had £60, and the lawyers the remaining £240. Of two counsel I employed, only one appeared; the other, however, stuck to his fee right enough. At the trial the judge sympathised very much with me, saying that, instead of being made to pay, I ought to have been rewarded for saving the life of the boy, and perhaps that of a lot of other people. He, however, had to administer the law as he found it, and I was responsible for any dangerous consequences brought about in my business. He suggested, however, as there was not much hurt done to the boy, to put down the damages as low as possible. The jury named £50, the sum I had originally offered to the boy's father of my own good will. The costs were four times that amount. I was fortunate, however, to find a purchaser for my tiger a few days after the accident; for Mr Edmonds, proprietor of Wombwell's Menagerie, having read the report in the papers, came up to town post haste, and paid me £300 for the tiger. He exhibited him as the tiger that swallowed the child, and by all accounts made a small fortune with him.

From *The Boy's Own Paper*, 1879

Two guineas reward

Lost on Sunday Night, about Nine of the Clock, from

my Lady Gouvernet in St James's Square, a Dutch Mastiff about 8 Years old, short Legg'd, with a large Neck and Head, pretty fat, big-eyed, short Nose and wide Mouth, his Back black, his belly, Breast, and Neck, Cream colour, with a black circle about his Neck, like a Collar exactly; and when he goes he straddles, and paws with his four Feet. Whoever brings him to my Lady Gouvernet's House in St James's Square shall have a Guinea and Reasonable Charges.

Post Boy, February, 1701

Henry Mayhew on dog theft

The difficulty of proving the positive theft of a dog was extreme. In most cases, where the man was not seen actually to seize a dog which could be identified, he escaped when carried before a magistrate. 'The dog-stealers,' said Inspector Shackell, 'generally go two together; they have a piece of liver; they say it is merely bullock's liver, which will entice or tame the wildest or savagest dog which there can be in any yard; they give it to him, and take him from his chain. At other times,' continues Mr Shackell, 'they will go in the street with a little dog, rubbed over with some sort of stuff, and will entice valuable dogs away. If there is a dog lost or stolen, it is generally known within five or six hours where that dog is, and they know almost exactly what they can get for it, so that it is a regular system of plunder.' Mr G. White, 'dealer in live stock, dogs, and other animals,' and at one time a 'dealer in lions, and tigers, and all sorts of things,' said of the dog-stealers: 'In turning the corners of streets there are two or three of them together; one will snatch up a dog and put into his apron, and the others will stop the lady and say, "What is the matter?" and direct the party who has lost the dog in a contrary direction to that taken.'

In this business were engaged from 50 to 60 men, half of them actual stealers of the animals. The others were the receivers, and the go-betweens or 'restorers.' The thief kept the dog perhaps for a day or two at some public-house, and he then took it to a dog-dealer with whom he was connected in the way of business. These dealers carried on a trade in 'honest dogs,' as one of the witnesses styled them (meaning dogs honestly acquired), but some of them dealt principally with the dog-stealers. Their depots could not be entered by the police, being private premises, without a search-warrant—and direct evidence was necessary to obtain a search-warrant—and of course a stranger in quest of a stolen dog would not be admitted. Some of the dog-dealers would not purchase or receive dogs known to have been stolen, but others bought and speculated in them. If an advertisement appeared offering a reward for the dog, a negotiation was entered into. If no reward was offered, the owner of the dog, who was always either known or

made out, was waited upon by a restorer, who un-
dertook 'to restore the dog if terms could be come
to.' A dog belonging to Colonel Fox was once kept
six weeks before the thieves would consent to the
Colonel's terms. One of the most successful restorers
was a shoe-maker, and mixed little with the actual
stealers; the dog-dealers, however, acted as restorers
frequently enough. If the person robbed paid a good
round sum for the restoration of a dog, and paid it
speedily, the animal was almost certain to be stolen a
second time, and a higher sum was then demanded.
Sometimes the thieves threatened that if they were
any longer trifled with they would inflict torture on
the dog, or cut its throat. One lady, Miss Brown of
Bolton-street, was so worried by these threats, and
by having twice to redeem her dog, 'that she has left
England,' said Mr Bishop, 'and I really do believe for
the sake of keeping the dog.' It does not appear, as far
as the evidence shows, that these threats of torture or
death were ever carried into execution; some of the
witnesses had merely heard of such things.

From *London Labour and the London Poor*, 1851

Thomas Pennant on the Earl of Southampton's cat

A very remarkable accident befell Henry Wriothes-
ley, Earl of Southampton, the friend and companion
of the Earl of Essex in his fatal insurrection: after he
had been confined [in the Tower of London] a small

time, he was surprised by a visit from his favourite cat, which had found its way to the Tower; and, as tradition days, reached its master by descending the chimney of his apartment. I have seen at Bulstrode, the summer residence of the late Duchess of Portland, an original portrait of this earl, in the place of his confinement, in a black dress and cloak, with the faithful animal sitting by him Perhaps this picture might have been the foundation of the tale.

From *Of London*, 1790

Hodge shan't be shot

I never shall forget the indulgence with which [Dr Johnson] treated Hodge, his cat: for whom he himself used to go out and buy oysters, lest the servants having that trouble should take a dislike to the poor creature. I am, unluckily, one of those who have an antipathy to a cat, so that I am uneasy when in the room with one; and I own, I frequently suffered a good deal from the presence of this same Hodge. I recollect him one day scrambling up Dr Johnson's breast, apparently with much satisfaction, while my friend smiling and half-whistling, rubbed down his back, and pulled him by the tail; and when I observed he was a fine cat, saying, 'Why yes, Sir, but I have had cats whom I liked better than this'; and then as if perceiving Hodge to be out of countenance, adding, 'but he is a very fine cat, a very fine cat indeed.'

This reminds me of the ludicrous account which he gave Mr Langton, of the despicable state of a young gentleman of good family. 'Sir, when I heard of him last, he was running about town shooting cats.' And then in a sort of kindly reverie, he bethought himself of his own favourite cat, and said, 'But Hodge shan't be shot; no, no, Hodge shall not be shot.'

From James Boswell, *Life of Johnson*, 1791

Human 'animals' at Bedlam

Bethlem Hospital was founded in 1547, and the early treatment of the miserable creatures committed to its brutal rulers appears to have been characterised by utter indifference to the feelings and comforts of the patients, and a studied aggravation of their miseries. Indeed, to our shame be it recorded, these miseries were made the materials for actual profit to the hospital; a sum of about £400 being annually collected by exhibiting the poor maniacs, chiefly naked, and uniformly chained to the walls of their dungeons, and by exciting them to the most violent manifestations of their maladies. This practice of showing the patients, like wild beasts, was abolished in 1770, but the abolition was unaccompanied by any other improvement in their treatment. Recently, however, the unfortunate lunatics have been more humanely treated.

From *The Pictorial Handbook of London*, 1854

DANDIES

At the west end of Jermyn Street, at the entrance to the Piccadilly Arcade, is a statue of the celebrated dandy Beau Brummell (1778–1840). It is largely thanks to him that London tailoring, marked by its consistent exuberance and attention to detail, continues to attract customers from all over the world. The tailors, shirt-makers and bootmakers of St James's and Mayfair continue to prosper and have made few significant concessions to modern taste. Brummell is their *genius loci*. His world, that of the high Regency, is described here by Captain Rees Howell Gronow (1794–1865), who knew him well and witnessed his rise and fall at first hand. From Gronow we learn that he truly was an initiator rather than a follower of fashion, his designs being carefully thought-out adaptations of the costume of the day, made to his specifications by his talented tailor, a Mr Weston, on Old Bond Street. Brummell's sartorial philosophy was founded on simplicity and cleanliness: 'clean linen and plenty of it' was one of his memorable utterances and he was known for appearing dressed from head to toe in spotless white linen, silk and cambric. He sent his laundry to Sussex and it came back to the metropolis fragrant with the scent (in the appropriate season) of fresh mown hay.

Captain Rees Howell Gronow is an invaluable and entertaining narrator of life in Regency London. His own
career was, perhaps, even more diverting than Brummell's, the ups and downs far outstripping the antics of
many a real or fictional rake of the period. Gronow had
been at Eton with Shelley: he had served in the Welsh
Guards having won the price of a horse, uniform and
commission at cards: he spent some time in a debtor's
prison: he was for a while a well-meaning but ineffec-
tual Member of Parliament: he was married twice, first
to a dancer from the Paris Opéra and then to a Bre-
ton aristocrat. The following extracts from his memoirs
recreate the exclusive atmosphere of Mayfair and Piccadilly. We learn that in those days a 'tacit understanding'
prevented the lower and middle classes from intruding
into Hyde Park. Gronow describes not only Brummell
but other leading dandies of the period.

R.D. Blumenfeld (1864–1948) was an American-born
journalist who first came to England in 1887 to cover
Queen Victoria's Golden Jubilee and ended his career
as editor of Lord Beaverbrook's *Daily Express*, a post he
held from 1902–32. His diary is a valuable source of
information about some of the quirkier aspects of London life, one of which, related here, was the enterpris-
ing way in which troopers of the Household Cavalry—
dandies to a man despite being ordinary soldiers of the
rank and file—supplemented the Queen's Shilling.

D'Arcy Honeybunn, the 'playboy of the demi-world',

is an enduring dandy, a creation of the South African poet and novelist William Plomer (1903–73), the publisher's reader at Jonathan Cape who discovered the Diaries of Francis Kilvert. Plomer moved to England in 1929 and quickly became part of a literary set that included Stephen Spender, Virginia Woolf and Elizabeth Bowen. He spotted very early in their careers the potential of such authors as Ian Fleming, Arthur Koestler, Ted Hughes, Stevie Smith, John Betjeman, Vladimir Nabokov, John Fowles and Alan Paton. Sadly, his own work never enjoyed the critical status it deserved and he gradually turned away from fiction towards engaging memoir and reminiscence.

The 'philosophy' of the dandy—diluted versions of which can be found in hundreds of fashion magazines and self-help books to this day—is captured in Chapter 44 of Edward Bulwer-Lytton's *Pelham*, a description of the hero being measured up by his tailor followed by a selection of his 'Maxims' for the guidance of the would-be well-dressed man. Lord Lytton (1803–75) was a fashionable and prolific author remembered today, perhaps rather unjustly, solely for a handful of phrases from his plays and novels that have passed into common usage: 'the great unwashed' (*Paul Clifford*, 1830), the 'pursuit of the almighty dollar' (*The Coming Race*) and 'the pen is mightier than the sword' (*Richelieu*). There is, sponsored by the English Department of San José State University, California, an annual Bulwer-Lytton Fiction Contest in which entrants are invited to compose 'the opening sentence to the worst of all possible novels'. The inspiration for this contest is the opening of Lytton's *Paul Clifford*, which many readers may feel has been unjustly maligned: 'It was a dark and stormy night; the rain fell in torrents—except at occasional intervals, when it was checked by a violent gust of wind which swept up the streets (for it is in London that our scene lies), rattling along the housetops, and fiercely agitating the scanty flame of the lamps that struggled against the darkness.'

The selection ends with an extract from *Evelina*, a novel-in-letters by Fanny Burney (1752–1840). The eponymous heroine meets a dandy at a private ball in London, but his sartorial showiness and *outré* manners fail to exert the effect he hoped for. The man is not so much a dandy as a coxcomb. True style, after all, must spring from within. It cannot be too much studied or contrived at.

Captain Gronow on the dandies of Hyde Park

That extensive district of park land, the entrances of which are in Piccadilly and Oxford Street, was far more rural in appearance in 1815 than at the present day. Under the trees cows and deer were grazing; the paths were fewer and none told of that perpetual tread of human feet which now destroys all idea of country charms and illusions. As you gazed from an eminence, no rows of monotonous houses reminded you of the vicinity of a large city, and the atmosphere of Hyde Park was then much more like what God has made it than the hazy, gray, coal-darkened half-twilight of the London of to-day. The company which then congregated daily about five, was composed of dandies and women in the best society; the men mounted on such horses as England alone could then produce. The dandy's dress consisted of a blue coat with brass buttons, leather breeches, and top boots; and it was the fashion to wear a deep, stiff white cravat, which prevented you from seeing your boots while standing. All the world watched Brummell to imitate him, and order their clothes of the tradesman who dressed that sublime dandy. One day a youthful beau approached Brummell and said, 'Permit me to ask you where you get your blacking?' 'Ah!' replied Brummell, gazing complacently at his boots, 'my blacking positively ruins me. I will tell you in confidence; it is made with the finest champagne!'

Captain Gronow on the fall of Beau Brummell

The Prince of Wales sent for Brummell, and was so much pleased with his manner and appearance, that he gave him a commission in his own regiment, the 10th Hussars. Unluckily, Brummell, soon after joining his regiment, was thrown from his horse at a grand review at Brighton, when he broke his classical Roman nose. This misfortune, however, did not affect the fame of the beau; and although his nasal organ had undergone a slight transformation, it was forgiven by his admirers, since the rest of his person remained intact. When we are prepossessed by the attractions of a favourite, it is not a trifle that will dispel the illusion; and Brummell continued to govern society, in conjunction with the Prince of Wales. He was remarkable for his dress, which was generally conceived by himself; the execution of his sublime imagination being carried out by that superior genius, Mr Weston, tailor, of Old Bond Street. The Regent sympathised deeply with Brummell's labours to arrive at the most attractive and gentlemanly mode of dressing the male form, at a period when fashion had placed at the disposal of the tailor the most hideous material that could possibly tax his art. The coat may have a long tail or a short tail, a high collar or a low collar, but it will always be an ugly garment. The modern hat may be spread out at the top, or narrowed, whilst the brim may be turned up or turned down, made a little wider or a little more narrow, still it is inconceivably hideous. Pantaloons and Hessian boots were the least objectionable features of the costume which the imagination of a Brummell and the genius of a Royal Prince were called upon to modify or change. The hours of meditative agony which each dedicated to the odious fashions of the day have left no monument save the coloured caricatures in which these illustrious persons have appeared.

Brummell, at this time, besides being the companion and friend of the Prince, was very intimate with the Dukes of Rutland, Dorset, and Argyll, Lords Sefton, Alvanley, and Plymouth. In the zenith of his popularity he might be seen at the bay window of White's Club, surrounded by the lions of the day, laying down the law, and occasionally indulging in those witty remarks for which he was famous. His house in Chapel Street corresponded with his personal 'get up'; the furniture was in excellent taste, and the library contained the best works of the best authors of every period and of every country. His canes, his snuff-boxes, his Sèvres china, were exquisite; his horses and carriage were conspicuous for their excellence; and, in fact, the superior taste of a Brummell was discoverable in everything that belonged to him.

But the reign of the king of fashion, like all other reigns, was not destined to continue for ever. Brummell warmly espoused the cause of Mrs Fitzherbert,

and this of course offended the Prince of Wales. I re-
fer to the period when his Royal Highness had abandoned that beautiful woman for another favourite. A
coldness sprang up between the Prince and his pro-
tégé, and finally, the mirror of fashion was excluded
from the royal presence. A curious accident brought
Brummell again to the dinner-table of his royal patron; he was asked one night at White's to take a hand
at whist, when he won from George Harley Drum-
mond £20,000. This circumstance having been related by the Duke of York to the Prince of Wales, the
beau was again invited to Carlton House. At the commencement of the dinner, matters went off smoothly;
but Brummell, in his joy at finding himself with his
old friend, became excited, and drank too much wine.
His Royal Highness—who wanted to pay off Brummell for an insult he had received at Lady Cholmonde-
ley's ball, when the beau, turning towards the Prince,
said to Lady Worcester, 'Who is your fat friend?'—had
invited him to dinner merely out of a desire for re-
venge. The Prince therefore pretended to be affronted
with Brummell's hilarity, and said to his brother, the
Duke of York, who was present, 'I think we had better
order Mr Brummell's carriage before he gets drunk.'
Whereupon he rang the bell, and Brummell left the
royal presence. This circumstance originated the story about the beau having told the Prince to ring the
bell. I received these details from the late General Sir

Arthur Upton, who was present at the dinner. The latter days of Brummell were clouded with mortifications and penury. He retired to Calais, where he kept up a ludicrous imitation of his past habits. At least he got himself named consul at Caen; but he afterwards lost the appointment, and eventually died insane, and in abject poverty, either at Boulogne or Calais.

From *The Reminiscences of Captain Gronow*, 1862

R.D. Blumenfeld on the gentlemen of the Guards

There was present at luncheon a tall, extremely well-dressed young man, with whom I returned to town in a hansom cab. I noticed that part of his forehead was very much sunburned, but one part, from the hair to the nose above the right eye, was of a different colour. This is 'the swagger mark' indicating a soldier. It comes from the pill-box, which protects only a small portion of the head and forehead from the sun; a much-coveted distinction. On the way he told me that he is a private in the 2nd Life Guards, and that 'the gentlemen of the Guards' are permitted to go off duty in mufti if they so desire. A large number of these Guardsmen, however, prefer to go out in uniform, shell jacket, very tight overalls, and pill-box askew on head, ready to be hired for an afternoon or evening by nursemaids to 'walk out'. There is a regular, fixed tariff. Household Cavalry for afternoon out in Park, half-a-crown and beer. Brigade of

Foot Guards, eighteen pence and beer. Royal Horse
Artillery, two shillings. Other services, a shilling. The
fact that there is a big demand is shown by the large
number of females at barrack gates early in the afternoon and evening waiting to engage escorts.

From the *Diary*, June 27th 1887

William Plomer: *The Playboy of the Demi-World* (1938)

Aloft in Heavenly Mansions, Doubleyou One—
Just Mayfair flats, but certainly sublime—
You'll find the abode of D'Arcy Honeybunn,
A rose-red sissy half as old as time.

Peace cannot age him, and no war could kill
The genial tenant of those cosy rooms,
He's lived there always and he lives there still,
Perennial pansy, hardiest of blooms.

There you'll encounter aunts of either sex,
Their jokes equivocal or over-ripe,
Ambiguous couples wearing slacks and specs
And the stout Lesbian knocking out her pipe.

The rooms are crammed with flowers and
objets d'art,
A Ganymede still hands the drinks—and plenty!
D'Arcy still keeps a rakish-looking car
And still behaves the way he did at twenty.

A ruby pin is fastened in his tie,
The scent he uses is Adieu Sagesse,
His shoes are suede, and as the years go by
His tailor's bill's not getting any less.

He cannot whistle, always rises late,
Is good at indoor sports and parlour-tricks,
Mauve is his favourite colour, and his gait
Suggests a peahen walking on hot bricks.

He prances forward with his hands outspread
And folds all comers in a gay embrace,
A wavy toupée on his hairless head,
A fixed smile on his often-lifted face.

'My dear!' he lisps, to whom all men are dear,
'How perfectly enchanting of you!' turns
Towards his guests and twitters, 'Look who's here!
Do come and help us fiddle while Rome burns!'

'The kindest man alive,' so people say,
'Perpetual youth!' But have you seen his eyes?
The eyes of some old saurian in decay
That asks no questions and is told no lies.

Under the fribble lurks a worn-out sage
Heavy with disillusion, and alone;
So never say to D'Arcy, 'Be your age!'—
He'd shrivel up at once or turn to stone.

Edward Bulwer-Lytton on tailors

'We are a very good figure, Mr Pelham; very good figure,' replied the Schneider, surveying me from head to foot, while he was preparing his measure; 'we want a little assistance though; we must be padded well here; we must have our chest thrown out, and have an additional inch across the shoulders; we must live for effect in this world, Mr Pelham; a leetle tighter round the waist, eh?'

'Mr. N—,' said I, 'you will take, first, my exact measure, and, secondly, my exact instructions. Have you done the first?'

'We are done now, Mr Pelham,' replied my man-maker, in a slow, solemn tone.

'You will have the goodness then to put no stuffing of any description in my coat; you will not pinch me an iota tighter across the waist than is natural to that part of my body, and you will please, in your infinite mercy, to leave me as much after the fashion in which God made me, as you possibly can.'

'But, Sir, we must be padded; we are much too thin; all the gentlemen in the Life Guards are padded, Sir.'

'Mr N—,' answered I, 'you will please to speak of us, with a separate, and not a collective pronoun; and you will let me for once have my clothes such as a gentleman, who, I beg of you to understand, is not a Life Guardsman, can wear without being mistaken for a Guy Fawkes on a fifth of November.'

Mr N—looked very discomfited: 'We shall not be liked, Sir, when we are made—we sha'n't, I assure you. I will call on Saturday at 11 o'clock. Good morning, Mr Pelham; we shall never be done justice to, if we do not live for effect; good morning, Mr Pelham.'

Scarcely had Mr N— retired, before Mr—, his rival, appeared. The silence and austerity of this importation from Austria, were very refreshing after the orations of Mr N—.

'Two frock-coats, Mr—,' said I, 'one of them brown, velvet collar same colour; the other, dark grey, no stuffing, and finished by Wednesday. Good morning, Mr—.'

'Monsieur B—, un autre tailleur,' said Bedos, opening the door after Mr S.'s departure.

'Admit him,' said I. 'Now for the most difficult article of dress—the waistcoat.'

And here, as I am weary of tailors, let me reflect a little upon that divine art of which they are the professors. Alas, for the instability of all human sciences! A few short months ago, in the first edition of this memorable Work, I laid down rules for costume, the value of which, Fashion begins already to destroy. The thoughts which I shall now embody, shall be out of the reach of that great innovator, and applicable not to one age, but to all. To the sagacious reader, who has already discovered what portions of this work are writ in irony—what in earnest—I fearlessly com-

mit these maxims; beseeching him to believe, with
Sterne, that 'every thing is big with jest, and has wit
in it, and instruction too, if we can but find it out!'

From *Pelham*, 1828

A selection of Lord Lytton's maxims

◆ Never in your dress altogether desert that taste
which is general. The world considers eccentricity
in great things, genius; in small things, folly.

◆ Keep your mind free from all violent affections at
the hour of the toilet. A philosophical serenity is
perfectly necessary to success. Helvetius says, justly,
that our errors arise from our passions.

◆ To win the affection of your mistress, appear negligent in your costume—to preserve it, assiduous:
the first is a sign of the passion of love; the second,
of its respect.

◆ A man must be a profound calculator to be a con-
summate dresser. One must not dress the same,
whether one goes to a minister or a mistress, an avaricious uncle or an ostentatious cousin: there is no
diplomacy more subtle than that of dress.

◆ The handsome may be showy in dress, the plain
should study to be unexceptionable; just as in great

men we look for something to admire—in ordinary men we ask for nothing to forgive.

* There may be more pathos in the fall of a collar, or the curl of a lock, than the shallow think for. Should we be so apt as we are now to compassionate the misfortunes and to forgive the insincerity of Charles I, if his pictures had portrayed him in a bob wig and a pigtail? Van Dyck was a greater sophist than Hume.

* Dress contains the two codes of morality—private and public. Attention is the duty we owe to others—cleanliness that which we owe to ourselves.

* Dress so that it may never be said of you 'What a well dressed man!'—but, 'What a gentlemanlike man!'

* A very benevolent man will never shock the feelings of others by an excess either of inattention or display; you may doubt, therefore, the philanthropy both of a sloven and a fop.

* He who esteems trifles for themselves is a trifler—he who esteems them for the conclusions to be drawn from them, or the advantage to which they can be put, is a philosopher.

From *Pelham*, 1828

Fanny Burney's heroine at a London ball

I have just had my hair dressed. You can't think how oddly my head feels; full of powder and black pins, and a great cushion on the top of it. I believe you would hardly know me, for my face looks quite different to what it did before my hair was dressed. When I shall be able to make use of a comb for myself I cannot tell; for my hair is so much entangled, frizzled they call it, that I fear it will be very difficult...

We passed a most extraordinary evening. A private ball this was called, so I expected to have seen about four or five couple; but Lord! my dear Sir, I believe I saw half the world! Two very large rooms were full of company; in one were cards for the elderly ladies, and in the other were the dancers. My mamma Mirvan, for she always calls me her child, said she would sit with Maria and me till we were provided with partners, and then join the card-players.

The gentlemen, as they passed and repassed, looked as if they thought we were quite at their disposal, and only waiting for the honour of their commands; and they sauntered about, in a careless, indolent manner, as if with a view to keep us in suspense. I don't speak of this in regard to Miss Mirvan and myself only, but to the ladies in general: and I thought it so provoking, that I determined in my own mind that, far from humouring such airs, I would rather not dance at all, than with any one who would seem to think me

ready to accept the first partner who would conde-
scend to take me.

Not long after, a young man, who had for some
time looked at us with a kind of negligent imperti-
nence, advanced on tiptoe towards me; he had a set
smile on his face, and his dress was so foppish, that I
really believed he even wished to be stared at; and yet
he was very ugly.

Bowing almost to the ground with a sort of swing,
and waving his hand, with the greatest conceit, after a short and silly pause, he said, 'Madam—may I
presume?'—and stopped, offering to take my hand. I
drew it back, but could scarce forbear laughing. 'Allow me, Madam,' continued he, affectedly breaking
off every half moment, 'the honour and happiness—
if I am not so unhappy as to address you too late—to
have the happiness and honour—'

Again he would have taken my hand; but bowing
my head, I begged to be excused, and turned to Miss
Mirvan to conceal my laughter. He then desired to
know if I had already engaged myself to some more
fortunate man? I said No, and that I believed I should
not dance at all. He would keep himself he told me,
disengaged, in hopes I should relent; and then, uttering some ridiculous speeches of sorrow and disappointment, though his face still wore the same invari-
able smile, he retreated.

From *Evelina*, 1778

CRIME & PUNISHMENT

The opening extracts are three centuries apart and it is interesting to compare them. Many of the lowlifes enumerated in John Northbrooke's censorious account of Elizabethan London resurface in Henry Mayhew's classification of Victorian malefactors—and it is easy to think of examples of all of them, appropriately modified, alive and thriving in London's underworld today.

The fifteen-year-old highwayman Bernard Fink was hanged in Newgate in 1731. His confession was saved for posterity as the result of a striking phenomenon of the time, the right of the prison chaplain, or 'Ordinary' as he was known, to record and publish his accounts of the last days and hours of the condemned prisoners in his care. James Guthrie, during his incumbency as Ordinary, produced a series of vivid and moving accounts of which this is one of the more disturbing, given Bernard's age and, at the outset, his promising start in life.

The story from last days of the 'Hanging Judge', Judge Jeffreys comes from a Georgian guidebook to London by the Welsh naturalist Thomas Pennant (*see p. 182*).

William Blake's *Sick Rose* is followed by the description of a contaminated rose of a very different nature, by Clarence Rook (1862–1915), a writer and journalist who found his themes among London's criminal poor.

William Pett Ridge (1860–1930) offers a late 19th-century description of teenage girls behaving badly in his best-selling crime novel *Mord Em'ly*. Again there are echoes in modern life. Pett Ridge's 'Gilliken Girls' can be encountered on many a modern housing estate and would happily 'carve their 'nitials' on the face of an unwary passer-by.

Oscar Wilde, on his way to Reading Gaol in November 1895, was famously stranded for an eternal half-hour at Clapham Junction, a endurance test described here in a passage from *De Profundis*. After his release, he wrote to a friend of his concerns for the future: 'Yes, we shall win in the end; but the road will be long and red with monstrous martyrdoms.' Other martyrs were the often namelesss thousands send to the gallows or transported to the colonies for what were very minor crimes—petty theft, poaching, pickpocketing—committed out of hunger and desperation. In his famous novel *Moll Flanders*, in which a female miscreant recounts her story of penury, trickery, double-crossing and an eventual chance of a new start in America, Daniel Defoe lays the blame firmly at the door of a social system which offers no chance to people to better themselves.

The final extract introduces a different kind of crime: the fictional variety. Wilkie Collins's *The Moonstone*, which turns on the story of a mysterious Indian diamond, has been hailed as the first detective novel in the English language.

John Northbrooke inveighs against idleness

In the 13th and 18th years of [Queen Elizabeth's] gracious reign, two acts were made for idle, vagrant and masterless persons, that used to loiter and would not work: [they] should, for the first offence, have a hole burned through the gristle of one of [their] ears, of an inch compass and, for the second offence committed therein, to be hanged. If these and such like laws were executed justly, truly and severely (as they ought to be), without any respect of persons, favour, or friendship, this dung and filth of idleness would easily be rejected and cast out of this commonwealth; there would not be so many loitering, idle persons, so many ruffians, blasphemers and swingebucklers, so many drunkards, tosspots, whoremasters, dancers, fiddlers and minstrels, diceplayers and maskers, fencers, thieves, interlude players, cutpurses, cozeners, masterless servants, jugglers, rogues, sturdy beggars, counterfeit Egyptians &c as there are…if these dunghills and filth in common weals were removed, looked unto and clean cast out by the industry, pain and travail of those that are set in authority and have government.

From *A Treatise against Dicing, Dancing, Plays and Interludes, with other Idle Pastimes*, 1577

Henry Mayhew's classification of criminals

In the first place, then, the criminal classes are divisible into three distinct families, i.e., the beggars, the cheats, and the thieves.

Of the beggars there are many distinct species: (1) The naval and the military beggars; as turnpike sailors and 'raw' veterans. (2) Distressed operative beggars; as pretended starved-out manufacturers, or sham frozen-out gardeners, or tricky hand-loom weavers, &c. (3) Respectable beggars; as sham broken-down tradesmen, poor ushers or distressed authors, clean family beggars, with children in very white pinafores and their faces cleanly washed, and the ashamed beggars, who pretend to hide their faces with a written petition. (4) Disaster beggars; as shipwrecked mariners, or blown-up miners, or burnt-out tradesmen, and lucifer droppers. (5) Bodily afflicted beggars; such as those having real or pretended sores or swollen legs, or being crippled or deformed, maimed, or paralyzed, or else being blind, or deaf, or dumb, or subject to fits, or in a decline and appearing with bandages round the head, or playing the 'shallow cove', i. e., appearing half-clad in the streets. (6) Famished beggars; as those who chalk on the pavement, 'I am starving', or else remain stationary, and hold up a piece of paper before their face similarly inscribed. (7) Foreign beggars, who stop you in the street, and request to know if you can speak French; or destitute Poles, Indians, or Lascars, or Negroes. (8) Petty trading beggars; as tract sellers, lucifer match sellers, boot lace venders, &c. (9) Musical beggars; or those who play on some musical instrument, as a cloak for begging; as scraping fiddlers, hurdy-gurdy and clarionet players. (10) Dependents of beggars; as screevers or the writers of 'slums' (letters) and 'fakements' (petitions), and referees, or those who give characters to professional beggars.

The second criminal class consists of cheats, and these are subdivisible into: (1) Government defrauders; as 'jiggers' (defrauding the excise by working illicit stills), and smugglers who defraud the customs. (2) Those who cheat the public; as swindlers, who cheat those of whom they buy; and duffers and horse-chanters, who cheat those to whom they sell; and 'charley pitchers', or low gamblers, cheating those with whom they play; and bouncers and besters, who cheat by laying wagers; and flat catchers', or ring-droppers, who cheat by pretending to find valuables in the street; and bubble-men, who institute sham annuity offices or assurance companies; and douceur-men, who cheat by pretending to get government situations, or provide servants with places, or to tell persons of something to their advantage. (3) The dependents of cheats; as 'jollies' and 'magsmen', or the confederates of other cheats; and 'bonnets', or those who attend gaming tables; and referees, who give false characters to servants.

The last of the criminal classes are the thieves, who

admit of being classified as follows: (1) Those who plunder with violence; as 'cracksmen', who break into houses; 'rampsmen', who stop people on the highway; 'bludgers' or 'stick slingers', who rob in company with low women. (2) Those who hocus or plunder persons by stupefying; as 'drummers', who drug liquor; and 'bug-hunters', who plunder drunken men. (3) Those who plunder by stealth, as (i) 'mobsmen', or those who plunder by manual dexterity, like 'buzzers', who pick gentlemen's pockets; 'wires', who pick ladies' pockets; 'prop-nailers', who steal pins or brooches; and 'thumble screwers', who wrench off watches; and shoplifters, who purloin goods from shops; (ii) 'sneaksmen', or petty cowardly thieves, and of these there are two distinct varieties, according as they sneak off with either goods or animals. Belonging to the first variety, or those who sneak off with goods, are 'drag-sneaks', who make off with goods from carts or coaches; 'snoozers', who sleep at railway hotels, and make off with either apparel or luggage in the morning; 'sawney-hunters', who purloin cheese or bacon from cheesemongers' doors; 'noisy racket men', who make off with china or crockeryware from earthenware shops; 'snow-gatherers', who make off with clean clothes from hedges; 'cat and kitten hunters', who make off with quart or pint pots from area railings; 'area sneaks', who steal from the area; 'dead-lurkers', who steal from the passages of houses; 'till friskers', who make off with the contents of tills; 'bluey-hunters', who take lead from the tops of houses; 'toshers', who purloin copper from ships and along shore; 'star-glazers', who cut the panes of glass from windows; 'skinners', or women and boys who strip children of their clothes; and mudlarks, who steal pieces of rope, coal and wood from the barges at the wharves.

Those sneaks-men, on the other hand, who purloin animals, are either horse-stealers or 'woolly bird' (sheep) stealers, or deer-stealers, or dog stealers, or poachers, or 'lady and gentlemen racket-men', who steal cocks and hens, or cat-stealers or body snatchers.

Then there is still another class of plunderers, who are neither sneaks-men nor mobsmen, but simply breach-of-trust-men, taking those articles only which have been confided to them; these are either embezzlers, who rob their employers; or illegal pawners, who pledge the blankets &c, at their lodgings, or the work of their employers; dishonest servants, who go off with the plate, or let robbers into their master's houses, bill stealers, and letter stealers.

Beside these there are (4) the 'shoful-men', or those who plunder by counterfeits; as coiners and forgers of checks, and notes, and wills; and lastly we have (5) the dependents of thieves; as 'fences', or receivers of stolen goods; and 'smashers', or the utterers of base coin.

From *The Criminal Prisons of London*, 1862

An account of the crimes of Bernard Fink, a fifteen-year-old highwayman condemned to death

Bernard Fink [was] 15 years of age the 28th day of January last, of honest respected parents, who took care of his education at school and in religious principles. His father was from Lübeck, and having business abroad, left England some years ago, and his wife and family in great poverty. But Bernard having been a smart, well-looking boy, a gentleman of great honour took him home to his house and intended to have given him good education, having put him to a top boarding-school at the other end of the town, to be instructed in Latin, Greek, writing, accompts, &c. And that gentleman had the goodness to order him fine clothes, above his degree, and as he said, the servants respected him, and sometimes he went out in a chair with a footman attending him; and if he had been obedient and pleased his good master, he intended to breed him a gentleman and to get him provided for, having no children of his own. But all this extraordinary kindness and civility could not instill any principle of honour into Fink, his genius naturally leading him to vice and corruption. His first wrong step was to gaming houses, by the advice and in company of a footman, which when his patron heard of he disowned him; and Fink being left to himself, he went abroad to his father's friends in Germany, where he learned to speak High-Dutch, but although some of his relations (as he said) were eminent men, and willing and capable to do for him, yet he would not be managed by them, but chose to return to the company of his blackguards, whom he preferred to all others. This manner of life he began to follow about four years ago, after he left the school, and when he had gone several times between London and Lübeck; being grown up a little, he joined himself to a company of most notorious, impudent young street-robbers, though a little older than he. Having done a deal of mischief about the town, they hired horses and went to Windsor, each of them having his mistress to bear him company, and there they were taken up, and brought to London, where Fink, because of his youth, was allowed to be an evidence, upon which three others were executed in November last, as was said in the account of Yates, who was the other evidence. At first he denied the fact of which he was convicted, but Armstrong said that it was true, and then he finding that there was no expectation of life, owned it. He had a natural inclination to villainy and was irreclaimable. It was said that he said in the cells, if he were let out, he would go straight to his old trade. He was said to be much addicted to women. He drank and swore very much, and was most active and rude in robbing people. He seemed to have been a boy capable of business, but he had such a natural bias to vice that he employed all his wit the wrong way. They said that he was lately married in the Fleet, and that they drank so liberally at the wedding that he and his companions pawned all their pistols, and found it difficult to get money to relieve them. Bernard alleged these stories about women were only said of him for jest. When I examined and spoke to him, he wept like a child, as he often did in chapel. This boy was a sad instance of the depravity of human nature, destitute of the grace of God and left to itself; he declared that he believed in Christ his Saviour, repented of all his sins, and forgave all offences, as he hoped for pardon from God.

The following is an account of the robberies which were committed by Bernard Fink and his companions, viz:

The first robbery which I ever committed was in company with William Warrington, Hugh Morris and James Bryan, in King-street, Golden Square, where we stopped a coach and robbed an apothecary's wife, of the value of 10s. and 6d. The next was in the same street; we met a woman, and attacked her, who said she had been at a trial at Westminster; we took from her a crown, with a green purse; we asked her the reason why she had not more money about her, upon which she replied, she had paid all her money at Westminster among the lawyers…

About ten months ago, we attacked all comers and goers, in Bond-street, by Hanover-square; especially one that had been at sea with my companion, Johnson; but at that time he said he lived with Col. Chartres, as a butler. When we bid him stand, he asked us whether we were upon our fun, knowing of Johnson; we replied, You shall see whether we are upon fun, so immediately showed him our pistols, at which he making a noise, a gentleman's servant came out to his assistance, but we soon made him quiet, for we laid hold of him, and was going to rob him, but he begged very much, and said he was but a poor servant and had but a crown and a watch about him. We told him, If he would stand still and not stir, we would not hurt him; upon this the footman did comply, and stood and looked on all the time that we was robbing of Johnson's acquaintance, who said he was formerly a midshipman in the same ship with him.

The next night we met a Roman priest, in Hanover-street, by Hanover-square, as he was knocking at his own door; we pulled him off of the steps, and pushed him up against his own rails, when two servant maids on the other side of the way, looking out of their windows, and seeing what we was doing; they cried out, upon which Bryan stepped over with a pistol in his hand, and swore if they did not put down their windows, he would shoot them; the girls being frighted, put them down. Then we riffled Mr Priest, and we took from him a silver hilted sword, a silver watch, a green purse, with 10s. and 6d. in gold, and some silver; we likewise took a cane from him, but he begged we would be so kind as to return him his cane again; accordingly we did. Since I have been under my misfortunes, I sent to him, to let him know where I had pawned his watch, but he never came, it lying but for 15s. and I believe the watch to be worth 5 or 6 [pounds]. but the sword I sold to that honest watch-maker, near the Sun-Tavern in Fleet-street, for 18s.

The chief cause of my coming to this untimely end, and several more unhappy creatures' ruin, is owing to a public-house in St Lawrence-lane, St Giles's in the Fields; who countenances us in all our robberies, and likewise harbours us, whenever we have committed any. For in the back part of the house they have a place where there is several beds for us; and we can come in any hour of the night; and what we get we spend there upon vile women; when all is gone, they encourage us to turn out again; and this unhappy way of life we live, till we are brought to this ignominious death. I exhort all good people (especially the officers of those parishes, where there is such wicked houses, which I am afraid there is too many in the City of London) to get them suppressed; for many parents in this popular city, who have children, will be bound to pray for you.

I exhort more particularly, the officers of St Giles's

in the Fields, to get that house above-mentioned suppressed; for then gentlemen may go in more safety about their lawful business; and likewise in taking an airing to Hampstead or High-gate, without being so frequently attacked as they are.

There is one thing more, which would be very necessary to have suppressed, and prosecuted to the utmost severity of the law, that is persons who buys the goods of us, which we call LOCKS: There is one B——, a watchmaker in Fleet-street, a very remarkable man, he going almost double, with his two knees meeting; I am willing to describe him, that you may mark him from other men: I have sold him watches and swords many times, which I have taken from gentlemen. And likewise he keeps a house of ill-fame in Fetter-lane; to the great disturbance of his honest neighbours.

This I testify to be the truth of the above facts,
as I am a dying youth,
B. Fink.
At the Place of Execution

From the account of James Guthrie,
Chaplain of Newgate Prison, 1731

Thomas Pennant on prisoners in the Tower

The fallen lord chancellor [Judge Jeffreys], the cruel instrument of despotism under James II, died, imprisoned here, of a broken heart, aided by intemperance. He was first interred in the church belonging to the Tower [of London] and afterwards was removed to that of St Mary, Aldermanbury and deposited near the body of his rakish son, lord Wem. In my younger days, I have heard of a hard-hearted insult on this once great man, during his imprisonment. He received, as he thought, a present of Colchester oysters; and expressed great satisfaction at the thought of having some friend yet left: but, on taking off the top of the barrel, instead of the usual contents, appeared an halter! To conclude this melancholy list, I shall return to ancient times, to lament the sad fate of my countrymen, victims to English ambition [Pennant was Welsh]. Here was basely confined, by Henry III, my countryman Gryfydd, father of our last prince Llewelyn ap Gryffydd, who, impatient of imprisonment, attempted to escape by lowering himself from the walls: the line he was descending by broke, and, being of a great bulk, he was dashed to pieces, and perished in a most miserable manner.

From *Of London*, 1790

William Blake: *The Sick Rose*

O rose, thou art sick!
The invisible worm,
That flies in the night,
In the howling storm,

Has found out thy bed
Of crimson joy,
And his dark secret love
Does thy life destroy.

From *Songs of Experience*, 1794

Clarence Rook on drugged roses and cigars

'If you come across Lizzie an' she offered you a rose,'
he said, 'an' arst you to smell it, it wouldn't be worf
your while.'

'Why not?' I asked.

'Fiddled,' said young Alf.

'You mean—'

'Drugged, you unnerstand. You smell the rose, an'
in 'arf a mo you dunno anyfink more. See?'

Young Alf dived into an inner pocket, and brought
out something which he held in the palm of his hand.

'What you fink of that for a ceegar?' he said.

I took it from him, fingered it, smelt it.

'I don't see anything curious about it,' I said. 'It
seems to be an ordinary twopenny smoke. Cabbage,
with a bit of tobacco-leaf wrapped round. Eh?'

''Tain't,' said young Alf. 'Not be a long chalk. Like to
smoke it, jest a little bit of it?'

'I think I'd prefer one of my own,' I replied.

'You're about right,' said young Alf. 'It's a faked ceegar.'

'Drugged?'

Young Alf nodded, and returning the cigar carefully to his inner pocket, he leaned forward and dropped his voice to a hoarse whisper. 'There's been a lot o' talk about druggin' liquor in pubs, puttin' snuff in, y' know. Well, even if you got a mug that you fink you can skin easy, it ain't so easy to fiddle is drink in a bar where there's lots of uvver people; you can take it from me. It ain't the drink that gets fiddled. The way a mug gets struck senseless is be ceegars. And cigarettes. See?'

Young Alf sat back and regarded me obliquely. 'It wasn't on'y a week ago,' he continued, 'I come across a toff in a bar that was 'avin' a bit extry, an' gettin' extry good-natured wiv it. So course I got into conversation wiv 'im, an' 'e stood drinks. Wasn't boozed, 'e wasn't, an' I reckon 'e was pretty fly, cause 'e kep' 'is coat buttoned tight. On'y he was talkin' free about the brass 'e'd got. Says 'e could buy up the ole bar an' all the bleed'n' crowd in it. Well, I finks I must run froo 'im if I see me way, on'y I couldn't see no pals stannin' around, an' I couldn't see me way until sudden like it come into me 'ead 'ow to work the job. An' me wiv me ceegar in me pocket all the time! See?

Well, presently I brings out me ceegar an' offers it to him, be way of returnin' the compliment of the drink 'e'd stood. See? An' course 'e takes it an' lights up.

"That's a nice smoke," 'e says.

"Oughter be," I chips in. "It come a long way fore it got 'ere. You don't get a smoke like that every day of the week, an' countin' Sundays," I says. An' that was Gawd's trewth.'

The contortion of Young Alf's face denoted intense amusement.

'Well, fore long,' continued young Alf, 'the toff began to get queer in 'is 'ead. Cause, you unnerstand, it was a faked ceegar what I'd give 'im. So I looks round at the uvver people in the bar, an' I says that my fren's a bit overcome an' I fink I'll take 'im into the fresh air. See? An' wiv that out we goes togevver, me tellin' 'im 'ow the fresh air'll liven 'im up like. An' time I'd got a 'ansom an' put 'im inside, the job was worked. Went froo 'im, carm an' easy, I did, while we drove along. An' then, soon as we come to a pub that I knew was awright, I stopped the cab an' says I was goin' to get some brandy for my fren' that wasn't feelin' well. Course I nips froo an' out at the back.'

'And what happened to the man in the cab, and the cabman?' I asked.

'Never see eiver of em again,' said young Alf. 'Don't want to.'

'Let me see that cigar again,' I said.

He drew it out with great care, and handed it to me.

'I rather fancy I detect a curious perfume about it,' I said. 'Not very marked, but still—'

'Not if you was a bit boozed,' said young Alf.

'Where do you buy those cigars?' I asked.

Young Alf returned the cigar to his pocket, puffed his cheeks once, but said nothing.

There are some things that young Alf will not tell me. He will not tell me where you get drugged cigars. But he knows where they are to be bought, and he knows what you must ask for when you want them.

'What you got to be careful of,' said young Alf as we were parting, 'is flahers, an' ceegars. An' cigarettes,' he added, as he turned at the door.

From *The Hooligan Nights*, 1899

William Pett Ridge on gang warfare

'The forring foe,' said Miss Gilliken grimly, 'is approaching. The forring foe is going to get what-for within the space of fifteen minutes. The forring foe is going to get such a welting that in future it'll keep to its own n'i'bourhood, and not come interfering with other people.'

'Good!' remarked one of the girls approvingly.

'Pull their 'eads of 'air,' said Miss Gilliken advisingly, 'sso that it 'urts; scratch for all you're worth; write your 'nitials on their faces. And if I give the whistle, run off 'ome separate like mad. J'ear?'

The members of the Gilliken Gang re-tied their back hair in knots, fixed their hats, and secured the laces of their boots. Then, keeping well in the shade of the houses, they walked quietly, but briskly, eastward. The bright moon cast a shadow half-way across the pavement; the rest of the roadway it illuminated brightly. The gang sniffed now and again when some appetising scent of frying came from the small houses, but nothing was permitted to arrest the gang's progress. Miss Gilliken communicated her further instructions in a whisper, and the members repeated them to each other, pulling up their sleeves as they did so, and aiming blows at the air for the sake of practice. When, at one or two corners, they had to pass by a constable, the gang broke up and became, individuals, with no knowledge, and certainly no interest, concerning each other's existence, to become once more a gang when they were out of the policeman's sight. The warning for the temporary disbandment was always given quietly by Miss Gilliken herself...

From *Mord Em'ly*, 1901

We are the zanies of sorrow

Everything about my tragedy has been hideous, mean, repellent, lacking in style; our very dress makes us grotesque. We are the zanies of sorrow. We are clowns whose hearts are broken. We are specially designed to appeal to the sense of humour. On November 13th, 1895, I was brought down here from London. From two o'clock till half-past two on that day I had to stand on the centre platform of Clapham Junction in convict dress, and handcuffed, for the world to look at. I had been taken out of the hospital ward without a moment's notice being given to me. Of all possible objects I was the most grotesque. When people saw me they laughed. Each train as it came up swelled the audience. Nothing could exceed their amusement. That was, of course, before they knew who I was. As soon as they had been informed they laughed still more. For half an hour I stood there in the grey November rain surrounded by a jeering mob...

Oscar Wilde, from *De Profundis*, written 1897,
published 1905

Daniel Defoe on the causes of felony

My true name is so well known in the records or registers at Newgate, and in the Old Bailey, and there are some things of such consequence still depending there, relating to my particular conduct, that it is not be expected I should set my name or the account of my family to this work; perhaps, after my death, it may be better known; at present it would not be proper, no not though a general pardon should be issued, even without exceptions and reserve of persons or crimes.

It is enough to tell you, that as some of my worst comrades, who are out of the way of doing me harm (having gone out of the world by the steps and the string, as I often expected to go), knew me by the name of Moll Flanders, so you may give me leave to speak of myself under that name till I dare own who I have been, as well as who I am.

I have been told that in one of our neighbour nations, whether it be in France or where else I know not, they have an order from the king, that when any criminal is condemned, either to die, or to the galleys, or to be transported, if they leave any children, as such are generally unprovided for, by the poverty or forfeiture of their parents, so they are immediately taken into the care of the Government, and put into a hospital called the House of Orphans, where they are bred up, clothed, fed, taught, and when fit to go out, are placed out to trades or to services, so as to be well able to provide for themselves by an honest, industrious behaviour.

Had this been the custom in our country, I had not been left a poor desolate girl without friends, without clothes, without help or helper in the world, as was my fate; and by which I was not only exposed to very great distresses, even before I was capable either of understanding my case or how to amend it, but brought into a course of life which was not only scandalous in itself, but which in its ordinary course tended to the swift destruction both of soul and body.

But the case was otherwise here. My mother was

convicted of felony for a certain petty theft scarce worth naming, viz. having an opportunity of borrowing three pieces of fine holland of a certain draper in Cheapside. The circumstances are too long to repeat, and I have heard them related so many ways, that I can scarce be certain which is the right account.

However it was, this they all agree in, that my mother pleaded her belly, and being found quick with child, she was respited for about seven months; in which time having brought me into the world, and being about again, she was called down, as they term it, to her former judgment, but obtained the favour of being transported to the plantations, and left me about half a year old; and in bad hands, you may be sure...

From *Moll Flanders*, 1722

Wilkie Collins introduces a faint odour of musk

[From the diary of Miss Clack]

We will now follow Mr Godfrey home to his residence at Kilburn.

He found waiting for him, in the hall, a poorly clad but delicate and interesting-looking little boy. The boy handed him a letter, merely mentioning that he had been entrusted with it by an old lady whom he did not know, and who had given him no instructions to wait for an answer. Such incidents as these were not uncommon in Mr Godfrey's large experience as a promoter of public charities. He let the boy go, and opened the letter.

The handwriting was entirely unfamiliar to him. It requested his attendance, within an hour's time, at a house in Northumberland Street, Strand, which he had never had occasion to enter before. The object sought was to obtain from the worthy manager certain details on the subject of the Mothers'-Small-Clothes-Conversion-Society, and the information was wanted by an elderly lady who proposed adding largely to the resources of the charity, if her questions were met by satisfactory replies. She mentioned her name, and she added that the shortness of her stay in London prevented her from giving any longer notice to the eminent philanthropist whom she addressed.

Ordinary people might have hesitated before setting aside their own engagements to suit the convenience of a stranger. The Christian Hero never hesitates where good is to be done. Mr Godfrey instantly turned back, and proceeded to the house in Northumberland Street. A most respectable though somewhat corpulent man answered the door, and, on hearing Mr Godfrey's name, immediately conducted him into an empty apartment at the back, on the drawing-room floor. He noticed two unusual things on entering the room. One of them was a faint odour of musk and camphor. The other was an ancient Oriental manuscript, richly illuminated with Indian figures and devices, that lay open to inspection on a table.

He was looking at the book, the position of which caused him to stand with his back turned towards the closed folding doors communicating with the front room, when, without the slightest previous noise to warn him, he felt himself suddenly seized round the neck from behind. He had just time to notice that the arm round his neck was naked and of a tawny-brown colour, before his eyes were bandaged, his mouth was gagged, and he was thrown helpless on the floor by (as he judged) two men. A third rifled his pockets, and—if, as a lady, I may venture to use such an expression—searched him, without ceremony, through and through to his skin.

Here I should greatly enjoy saying a few cheering words on the devout confidence which could alone have sustained Mr Godfrey in an emergency so terrible as this. Perhaps, however, the position and appearance of my admirable friend at the culminating period of the outrage (as above described) are hardly within the proper limits of female discussion. Let me pass over the next few moments, and return to Mr Godfrey at the time when the odious search of his person had been completed. The outrage had been perpetrated throughout in dead silence. At the end of it some words were exchanged, among the invisible wretches, in a language which he did not understand, but in tones which were plainly expressive (to his cultivated ear) of disappointment and rage. He was suddenly lifted from the ground, placed in a chair, and bound there hand and foot. The next moment he felt the air flowing in from the open door, listened, and concluded that he was alone again in the room.

An interval elapsed, and he heard a sound below like the rustling sound of a woman's dress. It advanced up the stairs, and stopped. A female scream rent the atmosphere of guilt. A man's voice below exclaimed 'Hullo!' A man's feet ascended the stairs. Mr Godfrey felt Christian fingers unfastening his bandage, and extracting his gag. He looked in amazement at two respectable strangers, and faintly articulated, 'What does it mean?' The two respectable strangers looked back, and said, 'Exactly the question we were going to ask *you.*'

From *The Moonstone*, 1868

FIRE & PLAGUE

The extracts in this chapter deal with fire and plague, both of which have visited London intermittently throughout its history. Defoe, Nashe and Evelyn were witnesses and Evelyn (*see p. 14*) played an important role in rebuilding London after the Great Fire of 1666. The diarist Samuel Pepys's (1633–1703) first-hand accounts of the Great Fire also provide valuable documentary evidence of how the citizens of London reacted to the calamity. Throughout the Diary he refers to no fewer than 15 serious fires, evidence enough that London's crowded, timber-framed houses were a serious fire risk.

The Bubonic Plague attacked London intermittently from the Middle Ages onwards. As the city rapidly expanded, sanitary conditions became increasingly dire as a result of overcrowding. The narrow streets with their open sewers were the ideal breeding grounds for the intensely contagious plague virus. Thomas Nashe (*bap.* 1567, *d. c.*1601) was a writer and dramatist from Lowestoft in Suffolk, an engaging stylist, typical of those who create in their prose the uncanny impression that they are virtually standing at the reader's side: 'I have heard aged mumping beldams as they sat warming their knees over a coal...When I was a little child I was a great auditor of theirs, and had all their witchcrafts at my fingers ends, as perfit as good morrow and good even,' he relates of his country childhood in Suffolk. His work is an entertaining source of strange usages: 'mingo', meaning a drunk (some say from San Domingo, the patron saint of tipplers) and 'pupillonian', one who squawks like peacock. his *Litany in Time of Plague* is a memorable and moving incantation.

Daniel Defoe (?1660–1731) was a writer and businessman, mainly remembered today for his bestselling classic *Robinson Crusoe* (1719), a fictional account of a man stranded on a desert island. The arrival of a native islander, Friday, enlivens the narrative and serves as a neat literary device by which to explore the questions raised by Crusoe's reflections on his—and all men's—place and duty in the world. Defoe's *Journal of the Plague Year* is an historical novel set against the London plague of 1665, though it is often mistakenly read as a work of journalistic non-fiction (there were those who believed *Robinson Crusoe* to be a true account as well). The passage is a remarkable exploration of naked and unconsolable grief and the compassion with which it is met by the very ordinary (they are gravediggers) protagonists in the story.

John Evelyn's accounts of the Great Fire

The burning still rages; I went now on horseback, & it was now gotten as far as the Inner Temple, all Fleet-street, Old Bailey, Ludgate Hill, Warwick-lane, Newgate, Paul's Chain, Watling-street now flaming & most of it reduced to ashes, the stones of Paul's flew like granados, the lead melting down the streets in a stream, & the very pavements of them glowing with a fiery redness, so as nor horse nor man was able to tread on them, & the demolitions had stopped all the passages, so as no help could be applied; the easter[n] wind still more impetuously driving the flames forwards. Nothing but the almighty power of God was able to stop them, for vain was the help of man: on the fifth it crossed towards White-hall, but oh, the confusion was then at that Court.

It pleased his Majesty to command me among the rest to look after the quenching of Fetter-lane end, to preserve (if possible) that part of Holborn, whilst the rest of the Gent. took their several posts, some at one part, some at another, for now they began to bestir themselves, & not 'til now, who 'til now had stood as men interdict, with their hands a-cross, & began to consider that nothing was like to put a stop, but the blowing up of so many houses, as might make a [wider] gap, than any had yet been made by the ordinary method of pulling them down with engines. This some stout seamen proposed early enough to

have saved the whole City. But some tenacious &
avaricious men, aldermen &c would not permit, because their houses must have been [of] the first. It
was therefore now commanded to be practised, &
my concern being particularly for the hospital of St
Bartholomeus near Smithfield, where I had many
wounded & sick men, made me the more diligent to
promote it; nor was my care for the Savoy less. So as
it pleased Almighty God by abating of the wind, &
the industry of people, now when all was lost, infus-
ing a new spirit into them (& such as had, if exerted
in time, undoubtedly preserved the whole) that the
fury of it began sensibly to abate, about noon, so as it
came no farther than the Temple westward, nor than
the entrance of Smithfield north; but continued all
this day & night so impetuous toward Cripple-gate,
& the Tower, as made us even all despair. It also brake
out again in the Temple: but the courage of the multitude persisting, & innumerable houses blown up
with gunpowder, such gaps & desolations were soon
made, as also by the former three days consumption,
as the back fire did not so vehemently urge upon the
rest, as formerly.

There was yet no standing near the burning &
glowing ruins near a furlong's space; the coal & wood
wharves & magazines of oil, rosin, &c did infinite
mischief; so as the invective I but a little before dedicated to his Majesty & published, giving warning

what might probably be the issue of suffering those shops to be in the City, was looked on as prophetic. But there I left this smoking & sultry heap, which mounted up in dismal clouds night & day, the poor inhabitants dispersed all about St George's, Moorfields, as far as Highgate, & several miles in circle, some under tents, others under miserable huts and hovels, without a rag, or any necessary utensils, bed or board, who from delicateness, riches & easy accommodations in stately & well-furnished houses, were now reduced to extremest misery & poverty. In this calamitous condition I returned with a sad heart to my house, blessing & adoring the distinguishing mercy of God, to me & mine, who in the midst of all this ruin, was like Lot, in my little Zoar, safe and sound.

From the *Diary*, 4th September 1666

I went this morning on foot from Whitehall as far as London Bridge, thro' the late Fleet-street, Ludgate hill, by St Paul's, Cheapside, Exchange, Bishopsgate, Aldersgate, & out to Moorfields, thence thro' Cornhill, &c with extraordinary difficulty, clambering over mountains of yet smoking rubbish, & frequently mistaking where I was, the ground under my feet so hot as made me not only sweat, but even burnt the soles of my shoes, & put me all over in sweat. In the meantime his Majesty got to the Tower by water, to demolish the houses about the Graft, which being built entirely about it, had they taken fire & attacked the White Tower where the magazines of powder lay, would undoubtedly have not only beaten down & destroyed all the bridge, but sunk & torn all the vessels in the river & rendered the demolition beyond all expression for several miles even about the country at many miles distance.

At my return I was infinitely concerned to find that goodly church St Paul's now a sad ruin, & that beautiful portico (for structure comparable to any in Europe, as not long before repaired by the late King) now rent in pieces, flakes of vast stone split in sunder, & nothing remaining entire but the inscription in the architrave, which showing by whom it was built had not one letter of it defaced: which I could not but take notice of. It was astonishing to see what immense stones the heat had in a manner calcined, so as all the ornaments, columns, friezes, capitals & projectures of massy Portland stone flew off, even to the very roof, where a sheet of lead covering no less than 6 acres by measure, being totally melted, the ruins of the vaulted roof, falling, brake into St Faith's, which being filled with the magazines of books, belonging to the Stationer[s], & carried thither for safety, they were all consumed burning for a week following. It is also observable that the lead over the altar at the east end was untouched; and among the divers monuments, the body of one bishop remained entire.

Thus lay in ashes that most venerable church, one of the ancientest pieces of early piety in the Christian world, beside near 100 more. The lead, ironwork, bells, plate &c melted; the exquisitely wrought Mercers' Chapel, the sumptuous Exchange, the august fabric of Christ Church, all the rest of the Companies' Halls, sumptuous buildings, arches, entries, all in dust. The fountains dried up & ruined, whilst the very waters remained boiling; the voragos of subterranean cellars, wells & dungeons, formerly warehouses, still burning in stench & dark clouds of smoke like hell, so as in five or six miles traversing about, I did not see one load of timber unconsumed, nor many stones but what were calcined white as snow, so as the people who now walked about the ruins appeared like men in some dismal desert, or rather in some great City, laid waste by an impetuous & cruel enemy, to which was added the stench that came from some poor creatures' bodies, beds & other combustible goods.

From the *Diary*, 7th September 1666

I went again to the ruins, for it was now no longer a City.

From the *Diary*, 10th September 1666

Samuel Pepys on London fires

This night my boy Wainman, as I was in my chamber, [I] overheard him let off some gunpowder; and hearing my wife chide him below for it, and a noise made, I call him up and find that it was powder that he had put in his pocket, and a match carelessly with it, thinking that it was out; and so the match did give fire to the powder and had burned his side and his hand, that he put into his pocket to put out the fire. But upon examination, and finding him in a lie about the time and place that he bought it, I did extremely beat him. And though it did trouble me to do it, yet I thought it necessary to do it.

> From the *Diary*, 2nd November 1661

Up and to the office, where we sat all the morning. At noon to the 'Change, after being at the Coffee-house, where I sat by Tom Killigrew, who told us of a fire last night in my Lady Castlemaine's lodging, where she bid £40 for one to adventure the fetching of a cabinet out, which at last was got to be done; and the fire at last quenched without doing much wrong.

> From the *Diary*, 26th January 1664

Thomas Nashe: *A Litany in Time of Plague* (1593)

Adieu, farewell, earth's bliss;
This world uncertain is;
Fond are life's lustful joys;
Death proves them all but toys;
I am sick, I must die.

Lord, have mercy on us!

Rich men, trust not wealth,
Gold cannot buy you health;
Physic himself must fade.
All things to end are made,
The plague full swift goes by;
I am sick I must die.
Lord, have mercy on us!

Beauty is but a flower
Which wrinkles will devour;
Brightness falls from the air;
Queens have died young and fair;
Dust hath closed Helen's eye.
I am sick, I must die.
Lord, have mercy on us!

Strength stoops unto the grave,
Worms feed on Hector brave;
Swords may not fight with fate,
Earth still holds ope her gate.
'Come, come!' the bells do cry.
I am sick, I must die.
Lord, have mercy on us!

Haste, therefore, each degree,
To welcome destiny;
Heaven is our heritage,

Earth but a player's stage;
Mount we unto the sky.
I am sick, I must die.
    Lord, have mercy on us!

Daniel Defoe on the London plague pits of 1665

There was nobody, as I could perceive at first, in the churchyard, or going into it, but the buriers and the fellow that drove the cart, or rather led the horse and cart; but when they came up to the pit they saw a man go to and again, muffled up in a brown cloak, and making motions with his hands under his cloak, as if he was in great agony, and the buriers immediately gathered about him, supposing he was one of those poor delirious or desperate creatures that used to pretend, as I have said, to bury themselves. He said nothing as he walked about, but two or three times groaned very deeply and loud, and sighed as he would break his heart.

When the buriers came up to him they soon found he was neither a person infected and desperate, as I have observed above, or a person distempered in mind, but one oppressed with a dreadful weight of grief indeed, having his wife and several of his children all in the cart that was just come in with him, and he followed in an agony and excess of sorrow. He mourned heartily, as it was easy to see, but with a kind of masculine grief that could not give itself vent by tears; and calmly defying the buriers to let him alone, said he would only see the bodies thrown in and go away, so they left importuning him. But no sooner was the cart turned round and the bodies shot into the pit promiscuously, which was a surprise to him, for he at least expected they would have been decently laid in, though indeed he was afterwards convinced that was impracticable; I say, no sooner did he see the sight but he cried out aloud, unable to contain himself. I could not hear what he said, but he went backward two or three steps and fell down in a swoon. The buriers ran to him and took him up, and in a little while he came to himself, and they led him away to the Pie Tavern over against the end of Houndsditch, where, it seems, the man was known, and where they took care of him. He looked into the pit again as he went away, but the buriers had covered the bodies so immediately with throwing in earth, that though there was light enough, for there were lanterns and candles in them, placed all night round the sides of the pit, upon heaps of earth, seven or eight, or perhaps more, yet nothing could be seen

From *A Journal of the Plague Year*, 1722

DEATH, BURIAL & BEYOND

The following selection begins with a pleasantly macabre paragraph by Henry James from *A London Life* (*see
p. 39*) in which the worldly and cynical Lady Davenant
invites her friends to look on her collection of photographs and paintings as a 'cemetery'.

Two accounts of funeral processions follow: the first,
by John Evelyn, records that of the unmourned Lord
Protector, Oliver Cromwell (d. 1658). The account of
Byron's funeral procession, a very different affair, is by
John Clare (1793–1864), a poet and farm labourer from
Northampton, who visited London on three occasions
in 1820, 1822 and 1824. His records of his visits are
offbeat and impressionistic, at their best immediately
memorable. The wistful sorrow of the young girl in the
crowd comes as no surprise, given what we know of the
enormous mystique that surrounded Byron by the time
of his death.

George Gordon Noel, sixth Baron Byron (1788–
1824) was an early victim of destructive criticism, his
first collection of poems having been roundly attacked
in the *Edinburgh Review* by the reformist lawyer and
politician Henry Brougham. Byron fought back, publishing in 1809 the well-received satirical poem *English
Bards and Scotch Reviewers*. The most glamorous of the

English 'Romantic' poets, Byron was described by his
mistress Lady Caroline Lamb as 'mad, bad and dangerous to know' and by himself as follows: 'there are two
sentiments to which I am constant: a strong sense of
liberty, and a detestation of cant, and neither is calculated to gain me friends.' There are many portraits of
him, but perhaps the most characteristic is the chalk
drawing by George Henry Harlow, with its ruby lips,
cool eyes, waving locks and finely-chiselled features:
it is easy to imagine this remorseless sensualist caus-
ing women to swoon, easy also to conjure the brave,
single-minded patrician who swam the Hellespont and
died at Missolonghi, fighting in the Greek struggle for
independence from Ottoman Turkey. Byron's political
views were revolutionary—he admired Napoleon, he
spoke out in the House of Lords against imposing the
death sentence on Luddites—but in the end, thanks
to a strong satirical bent, he had developed too great
a contempt for all systems of government to be truly
effective as a social reformer. Shelley reckoned him a
potential anarchist, but with the destructive 'canker of
aristocracy'. An enthusiastic and effective seducer, he
left in his wake angry husbands and fathers, inconsol-
able cast-off mistresses and a small clutch of male lov-
ers. He was educated at Harrow, then at Trinity College, Cambridge, where he kept a bear—an eccentricity
magnified in later life at Ravenna, where he kept eight
dogs, five cats, three monkeys, five peacocks, two hens,

an eagle, a crow, a falcon, a crane and a badger. Often in debt or at best seriously overstretched, in 1818 he was forced to sell the Byron ancestral home, Newstead Abbey in Nottinghamshire. He has consistently been honoured in Greece, very unevenly in England: in 1924 Bishop Ryle wrote that 'Byron, partly by his own openly dissolute life and partly by the influence of licentious verse, earned a worldwide reputation for immorality among English-speaking people. A man who outraged the laws of our Divine Lord, and whose treatment of women violated the Christian principles of purity and honour, should not be commemorated in Westminster Abbey.' It took the Swinging Sixties to soften the Church of England: Byron's tablet was fixed to the floor of Poet's Corner in Westminster Abbey in 1969.

James Payn (1830–98) was a novelist and journal editor probably best known, somewhat unjustly, for a quatrain he penned on the one obvious peril attendant on consuming toast:

> I never had a piece of toast
> Particularly long and wide,
> But fell upon the sanded floor,
> And always on the buttered side.

His account of a London funeral is chiefly notable for the presence of the professional mourner, a memorable character by any standards, an old black man with hair as 'white as wool' and a copious cambric handkerchief into which to weep.

Charlie Chaplin (1889–1977) endured a miserable childhood in Walworth, East London. His father Charles, whom he loved, was an alcoholic music hall performer who died early: the Evangelical priest's remorseless verdict is evenly noted by Chaplin in this moving passage. After his father's funeral, Chaplin hits upon the idea of selling narcissi in local pubs—the picture that is subsequently evoked of a wan little boy with a pleading, wide-eyed look prefigures his 'little tramp' film persona in the most unsettling way.

Bram Stoker's Lucy rests in the family vault in Hampstead, by a process of elimination identifiable as the still very beautiful churchyard of Hampstead Parish Church in Church Row. But she did not remain long in her vault: mysterious sightings of the 'Bloofer Lady' suggest that she quickly found a new vocation after death.

The novelist Henry Fielding (1707–54) offers an original view of what form life after death might take for a typical literary Londoner towards the middle of the 18th century. The depressing verdict is that one might have ended up a helpless witness to all the quotidian set-pieces of the day, among them the excessive consumption of gin and the sight of relatives quarrelling over legacies. Eventually he is directed to Warwick Lane by a benevolent porter, a figure intended to recall the mythological Hermes Psychopompos, conductor of souls to the Underworld. Warwick Lane, we learn, is the point of departure for the coach to the Other World. The postcode is EC4 and now, as then, Warwick Lane is close to the Old Bailey and Newgate, respectively London's lawcourt and prison, and once the scene of wholesale condemnation and execution.

The Swedish visionary Emanuel Swedenborg (1688–1772) proposes the intriguing idea that there are two Londons in the afterlife, one reserved for the virtuous (or at least for the pious) and the other a specially designed hell for the wicked. William Blake (1757–1827), who was familiar with Swedenborg's work, formed his own distinctive vision of London as the Heavenly City.

Wilfred Owen (1893–1918) is best remembered as a war poet. The London poem printed here is of considerable interest, being written in the last year of the poet's life (and of the First World War), though its subject has nothing to do with the conflict. It is a purely London piece, an evocation, humane and moving, of a street-walker of the East End, a figure who appears to many as no more than a flitting, incorporeal shadow, though she is fully alive and alert to feeling, conscious of her own disconnection, with 'tumultuous eyes' like the River Thames she walks beside, all through the long night, until daylight exorcises her. The poem clearly owes much to Wilde's *Impression du Matin* (*see p. 33*).

'Oh, it's a cemetery,' she said

Lady Davenant's bright drawing-room was filled with mementoes and especially with a collection of portraits of distinguished people, mainly fine old prints with signatures, an array of precious autographs. 'Oh, it's a cemetery,' she said, when the young man asked her some question about one of the pictures; 'they are my contemporaries, they are all dead and those things are the tombstones, with the inscriptions. I'm the grave-digger, I look after the place and try to keep it a little tidy. I have dug my own little hole,' she went on, to Laura, 'and when you are sent for you must come and put me in.'

From *A London Life*, 1887, by Henry James

John Evelyn at Cromwell's funeral procession

He was carried from Somerset House in a velvet bed of State drawn by six horses, houss'd with the same; the pall held up by his new lords; Oliver lying in effigy in royal robes, and crowned with a crown, sceptre, and globe, like a king. The pendants and guidions were carried by the officers of the army; and the imperial banner, achievement, &c, by the heralds in their coats; a rich caparisoned horse, embroidered all over with gold; a knight of honour armed *cap-à-pie*, and, after all, his guards, soldiers and innumerable mourners. In this equipage they proceeded to Westminster; but it was the joyfullest funeral I ever saw,

for there were none that cried but dogs, which the
soldiers hooted away with a barbarous noise, drinking and taking tobacco in the streets as they went.

From the *Diary*, November 1658

John Clare at the funeral procession of Lord Byron

While I was in London, the melancholy death of
Lord Byron was announced in the public papers, and
I saw his remains borne away out of the city on its
last journey to that place where fame never comes.
His funeral was blazed in the papers with the usual
parade that accompanies the death of great men. I
happened to see it by chance as I was wandering up
Oxford Street…when my eye was suddenly arrested
by straggling groups of the common people collected
together and talking about a funeral. I did as the rest
did, though I could not get hold of what funeral it
could be; but I knew it was not a common one by the
curiosity that kept watch on every countenance. By
and by the group collected into about a hundred or
more, when the train of a funeral suddenly appeared,
on which a young girl gave a deep sigh and uttered,
'Poor Lord Byron.' I looked up at the young girl's face.
It was dark and beautiful, and I could almost feel in
love with her for the sigh she had uttered for the poet;
it was worth all the newspaper puffs and magazine
mournings that ever were paraded. The common
people felt his merits and his power, and the com-

mon people of a country are the best feelings of a
prophecy of futurity. They are the veins and arteries
that feed and quicken the heart of living fame.

From the prose writings, 1824

James Payn at a first class interment

Thirty years ago, the last home of even a wealthy
Londoner was a crowded vault beneath some church
hemmed in by houses; while that of the poorer sort
could hardly be called a resting-place, since, sooner
or later, their bones had to make way for the more recently deceased, and were thrown to left and right by
the grave-digger. Higher and higher grew the half-hu-
man churchyard, shutting out window after window
of the many peopled houses round from outlook and
air, and substituting for the one a wall of rank rich
grass, whose greenness speaks not of life and spring-
time, but of death and corruption, and for the other,
the pestilence that walketh in the noonday and the
night alike. Even in the vaults of so-called fashionable churches, not only were no pains taken to render
death less abhorrent, but it was positively made more
hideous by circumstance. The tawdry pomp of crape
and baton, of pawing horses and nodding plumes,
and all the hired panoply of sorrow, went no further
than the grave's mouth.

I remember being present at a certain funeral in
those days—a 'first class interment', it was called,

in the jargon of the undertaker—where all the out-ward respect that could be provided for the sad occasion had been purchased without regard to expense. Gentlemen in dusky pairs, and overcome with costly emotion, preceded the long procession, each furnished with what looked like a folded telescope, as though they would have followed with their bodily eyes the supposed direction of the late flight of the fashionable spirit. Then a dusky gentleman alone, bearing a board upon his head with ostrich feathers on it, exactly as the Italian image-boys carry their frail wares. Then another group of telescope-bearers. Then a sort of (muffled) drum-major in the deepest mourning and despondency. After him the hearse itself, with a gentleman more than dusky—for he was a genuine black man—sitting beside the driver. The appearance of this person was calculated to excite sympathy even from the most callous spectator. He was bowed no less with years than with grief, and his short hair—which still retained the curl peculiar to his race—was as white as wool.

I inquired of a relative of the deceased person who this individual was, for I did not remember ever to have seen him in that gentleman's household.

'I dare say not,' returned he; 'for the fact is, I never set eyes on him myself before to-day. Mr Mole, however, assured us that it would be the correct thing to engage him. "An ancient and valued retainer of the family," said he, "is indispensable on such occasions as these, and a black man for this purpose is invaluable." He is set down in the estimate at £3 16s., exclusive of the cambric handkerchief—which, to do him justice, he applies to his eyes as continuously as is consistent with exhibiting his complexion to the general public.'

After the hearse came, of course, the mourning coaches, and a long train of private carriages, full, perhaps, of unmitigated grief—for there was nothing else in them. At the mouth of the dismal-looking vault we were all arranged in a certain order, while Mr Mole distributed among us little packets of lavender-coloured paper, which I took at first to contain sugar-plums, but which in reality held gravel, refined to the delicate consistency of cayenne-pepper. 'At the words "ashes to ashes, dust to dust",' whispered he to each of us with a solemn smirk, 'you will be so kind as to sprinkle the contents upon the coffin.'

And yet, I remember, when the grim pantomime was over, and the plumes were packed away, and the hired mourners (including the ancient retainer) consoling themselves for their bereavement in the neighbouring public-house, the coffin of the deceased person's late wife, who had been buried but a few years back with the like magnificence, and next to which he had wished his own to be laid, could nowhere be found. The relative before alluded to, and myself, had remained behind to see that this request was carried out, and but for us it would certainly have been disregarded. We descended into the vault, and only after several hours discovered what we sought. All the coffins, without the least regard to the relationship of their inmates, were bound up in bundles of half-a-dozen each, and fastened together by means of huge black chains. How wretched was such a resting-place, contrasted with a grave that 'takes the sunshine and the rains,' such as the very humblest can command in a village churchyard!

From *Lights and Shadows of London Life*, 1867

Charlie Chaplin on the death of his father

The Three Stags in the Kennington Road was not a place my father frequented, yet as I passed it one evening an urge prompted me to peek inside to see if he was there. I opened the saloon door just a few inches, and there he was, sitting in the corner! I was about to leave, but his face lit up and he beckoned me to him. I was surprised at such a welcome, for he was never demonstrative. He looked very ill, his eyes were sunken, and his body had swollen to an enormous size. He rested one hand, Napoleon-like, in his waistcoat as if to ease his difficult breathing. That evening he was most solicitous, enquiring after Mother and Sydney, and before I left took me in his arms and for the first time kissed me. That was the last time I saw him alive.

Three weeks later, he was taken to St Thomas's Hospital. They had to get him drunk to get him there. When he realised where he was, he fought wildly— but he was a dying man. Though still very young, only thirty-seven, he was dying of dropsy. They tapped sixteen quarts of liquid from his knee.

Mother went several times to see him and was always saddened by the visit. She said he spoke of wanting to go back to her and start life anew in Africa. When I brightened at such a prospect, Mother shook her head, for she knew better. 'He was saying that only to be nice,' she said.

One day she came home from the hospital indignant over what the Reverend John McNeil, Evangelist, had said when he paid Father a visit: 'Well, Charlie, when I look at you, I can only think of the old proverb: "Whatsoever a man soweth, that shall he also reap".'

'Nice words to console a dying man,' said Mother. A few days later Father was dead.

The hospital wanted to know who would bury him. Mother, not having a penny, suggested the Variety Artists' Benevolent Fund, a theatrical charity organisation. This caused an uproar with the Chaplin side of the family—the humiliation of being buried by charity was repugnant to them. An Uncle Albert from Africa, my father's youngest brother, was in London at the time and said he would pay for the burial.

The day of the funeral we were to meet at St Thomas's Hospital, where we were to join the rest of the Chaplins and from there drive out to Tooting Cemetery. Sydney could not come, as he was working. Mother and I arrived at the hospital a couple of hours before the allotted time because she wanted to see Father before he was enclosed.

The coffin was enshrouded in white satin and around the edge of it, framing Father's face, were little white daisies. Mother thought they looked so simple and touching and asked who had placed them there. The attendant told her that a lady had called early that morning with a little boy. It was Louise.

In the first carriage were Mother, Uncle Albert and me. The drive to Tooting was a strain, for she had never met Uncle Albert before. He was somewhat of a dandy and spoke with a cultured accent; although polite, his attitude was icy. He was reputed to be rich; he had large horse ranches in the Transvaal and had provided the British Government with horses during the Boer War.

It poured with rain during the service; the grave-diggers threw down clods of earth on the coffin which resounded with a brutal thud. It was macabre and horrifying and I began to weep. Then the relatives threw in their wreaths and flowers. Mother, having nothing to throw in, took my precious black-bordered handkerchief. 'Here, sonny,' she whispered, 'this will do for both of us.' Afterwards the Chaplins stopped off at one of their pubs for lunch, and before leaving asked us politely where we desired to be dropped. So we were driven home.

When we returned there was not a particle of food in the cupboard except a saucer of beef dripping, and Mother had not a penny, for she had given Sydney her last twopence for his lunch money. Since Father's illness she had done little work, and now, near the end of the week, Sydney's wages of seven shillings as a telegraph boy had already run out. After the funeral we were hungry. Luckily the rag-and-bone man was passing outside and we had an old oil stove, so reluctantly she sold it for a halfpenny and bought a halfpenny worth of bread to go with the dripping.

Mother, being the legal widow of my father, was told the next day to call at the hospital for his belongings, which consisted of a black suit spotted with blood, underwear, a shirt, a black tie, an old dressing-gown, and some plaid house slippers with oranges stuffed in the toes. When she took the oranges out, a half sovereign fell out of the slippers on to the bed. This was a godsend!

For weeks I wore crêpe on my arm. These insignia of grief became profitable when I went into business on a Saturday afternoon, selling flowers. I had persuaded Mother to loan me a shilling, and went to the flower market and purchased two bundles of narcissus, and after school busied myself making them into penny bundles. All sold, I could make a hundred percent profit.

I would go into the saloons, looking wistful, and whisper: 'Narcissus, miss!' 'Narcissus, madame!' The women always responded: 'Who is it, son?' And I would lower my voice to a whisper: 'My father,' and they would give me tips. Mother was amazed when I came home in the evening with more than five shillings for an afternoon's work. One day she bumped into me as I came out of a pub, and that put an end to my flower-selling; that her boy was peddling flowers in bar-rooms offended her Christian scruples. 'Drink killed your father, and money from such a source will only bring us bad luck,' she said. However, she kept the proceeds, though she never allowed me to sell flowers again.

From *My Autobiography*, 1964

The mystery of the Bloofer Lady

Lucy lies in the tomb of her kin, a lordly death house in a lonely churchyard, away from teeming London, where the air is fresh, and the sun rises over Hampstead Hill, and where wild flowers grow of their own accord…

THE WESTMINSTER GAZETTE, 25 SEPTEMBER
A HAMPSTEAD MYSTERY

The neighbourhood of Hampstead is just at present exercised with a series of events which seem to run on lines parallel to those of what was known to the writers of headlines as 'The Kensington Horror,' or 'The Stabbing Woman,' or 'The Woman in Black.' During the past two or three days several cases have occurred of young children straying from home or neglecting to return from their playing on the Heath. In all these cases the children were too young to give any properly intelligible account of themselves, but the consensus of their excuses is that they had been with a 'bloofer lady.' It has always been late in the evening when they have been missed, and on two occasions the children have not been found until early in the following morning. It is generally supposed in the neighbourhood that, as the first child missed gave as his reason for being away that a 'bloofer lady' had asked him to come for a walk, the others had picked up the phrase and used it as occasion served. This is the more natural as the favourite game of the little ones at present is luring each other away by wiles. A correspondent writes us that to see some of the tiny tots pretending to be the 'bloofer lady' is supremely funny. Some of our caricaturists might, he says, take a lesson in the irony of grotesque by comparing the reality and the picture. It is only in accordance with general principles of human nature that the 'bloofer lady' should be the popular role at these *al fresco* performances. Our correspondent naively says that even Ellen Terry could not be so winningly attractive as some of these grubby-faced little children pretend, and even imagine themselves, to be.

There is, however, possibly a serious side to the question, for some of the children, indeed all who have been missed at night, have been slightly torn or wounded in the throat. The wounds seem such as might be made by a rat or a small dog, and although of not much importance individually, would tend to show that whatever animal inflicts them has a system or method of its own. The police of the division have been instructed to keep a sharp lookout for straying children…in and around Hampstead Heath, and for any stray dog which may be about.

From *Dracula* by Bram Stoker, 1897

Henry Fielding has an out-of-body experience

On the first day of December 1741, I departed this life at my lodgings in Cheapside. My body had been some time dead before I was at liberty to quit it, lest it should by any accident return to life: this is an injunction imposed on all souls by the eternal law of fate, to prevent the inconveniences which would follow. As soon as the destined period was expired (being no longer than till the body is become perfectly cold and stiff) I began to move; but found myself under a difficulty of making my escape, for the mouth or door was shut, so that it was impossible for me to go out at it; and the windows, vulgarly called the eyes, were so closely pulled down by the fingers of a nurse, that I could by no means open them. At last I perceived a beam of light glimmering at the top of the house (for such I may call the body I had been inclosed in), whither ascending, I gently let myself down through a kind of chimney, and issued out at the nostrils.

No prisoner discharged from a long confinement ever tasted the sweets of liberty with a more exquisite relish than I enjoyed in this delivery from a dungeon wherein I had been detained upwards of forty years, and with much the same kind of regard I cast my eyes backwards upon it.

My friends and relations had all quitted the room, being all (as I plainly overheard) very loudly quarrelling below stairs about my will; there was only an old woman left above to guard the body, as I apprehend. She was in a fast sleep, occasioned, as from her savour it seemed, by a comfortable dose of gin. I had no pleasure in this company, and, therefore, as the window was wide open, I sallied forth into the open air: but, to my great astonishment, found myself unable to fly, which I had always during my habitation in the body conceived of spirits; however, I came so lightly to the ground that I did not hurt myself; and, though I had not the gift of flying (owing probably to my having neither feathers nor wings), I was capable of hopping such a prodigious way at once, that it served my turn almost as well. I had not hopped far before I perceived a tall young gentleman in a silk waistcoat, with a wing on his left heel, a garland on his head, and a caduceus in his right hand. I thought I had seen this person before, but had not time to recollect where, when he called out to me and asked me how long I had been departed. I answered I was just come forth. 'You must not stay here,' replied he, 'unless you have been murdered: in which case, indeed, you might have been suffered to walk some time; but if you died a natural death you must set out for the other world immediately.' I desired to know the way. 'O,' cried the gentleman, 'I will show you to the inn whence the stage proceeds; for I am the porter. Perhaps you never heard of me—my name is Mercury.' 'Sure, sir,' said I, 'I have seen you at the playhouse.' Upon which he smiled, and, without satisfying me as to that point, walked directly forward, bidding me hop after him. I obeyed him, and soon found myself in Warwick-lane; where Mercury making a full stop, pointed at a particular house, where he bade me enquire for the stage, and, wishing me a good journey, took his leave, saying he must go seek after other customers.

From *A Journey from This World to the Next*, 1749

Swedenborg on where Londoners go after death

There are two large cities like London, to which most

of the English go after death. I was permitted to see one of these and to walk through it. Where in London the merchants meet, which is called the Exchange, there in that city is the centre where its governors reside. Above that centre is the east, below it is the west; on the right is the south, and on the left the north. In the eastern quarter those dwell who have lived a life of charity in a greater degree than others; here are magnificent palaces. In the southern quarter the wise dwell, and among them there is much splendour. In the northern quarter those dwell who more than others have loved freedom of speech and the press. In the western quarter those dwell who deal in justification by faith alone. On the right in this latter quarter there is an entrance to the city and also an exit therefrom; and those who live wickedly are here put out of the city. The preachers who live in the western quarter and teach the doctrine of faith alone, do not dare to enter the city by the large streets, but only through the narrow alleys, because none but those who believe in charity are tolerated in the city proper. I have heard them complaining of the preachers from the west, that they composed their sermons with so much art and eloquence, secretly weaving into them the doctrine of justification by faith, that they did not know whether good ought to be done or not. They preach that faith inwardly is a good, and this good they distinguish from the good of charity, which they call good that claims a merit, and therefore not acceptable to God. But when those who dwell in the eastern and southern quarters of the city hear such sermons they leave the churches, and the preachers are afterward deprived of the priestly office.

The other large city called London is not in the Christian heartland, but remote from it to the north. To that come after death those who are inwardly wicked. At its centre there is an opening leading to hell, and from time to time people are swallowed up in it.

From *True Christian Religion*, 1786

William Blake's vision of London

The fields from Islington to Marybone,
To Primrose Hill and Saint Johns Wood:
   Were builded over with pillars of gold,
And there Jerusalem's pillars stood.

   Her little ones ran on the fields
The Lamb of God among them seen
   And fair Jerusalem his Bride:
Among the little meadows green.

   Pancras and Kentish-town repose
Among her golden pillars high:
   Among her golden arches which
Shine upon the starry sky.

From *Jerusalem*, 1804

Wilfred Owen: *Shadwell Stair* (1918)

I am the ghost of Shadwell Stair.
Along the wharves by the water-house,
And through the cavernous slaughter-house,
I am the shadow that walks there.

Yet I have flesh both firm and cool,
And eyes tumultuous as the gems
Of moons and lamps in the full Thames
When dusk sails wavering down the pool.

Shuddering the purple street-arc burns
Where I watch always; from the banks
Dolorously the shipping clanks
And after me a strange tide turns.

I walk till the stars of London wane
And dawn creeps up the Shadwell Stair.
But when the crowing sirens blare
I with another ghost am lain.

EPILOGUE

This poem, by James Elroy Flecker (1884–1915) sums up all of city life: love-making, romance in the face of penury, future plans and escapes from urban smog to rural beauty on the Heath. But on the dark side lurk loneliness, desertion, the flim-flam of bright lights, ill health. The poem ends with a blend of optimism and stoicism that city dwellers the world over will surely recognise.

The Ballad of Camden Town

I walked with Maisie long years back
The streets of Camden Town,
I splendid in my suit of black,
And she divine in brown.

Hers was a proud and noble face,
A secret heart, and eyes
Like water in a lonely place
Beneath unclouded skies.

A bed, a chest, a faded mat,
And broken chairs a few,
Were all we had to grace our flat
In Hazel Avenue.

But I could walk to Hampstead Heath,
And crown her head with daisies,
And watch the streaming world beneath,

And men with other Maisies.

When I was ill and she was pale
And empty stood our store,
She left the latchkey on its nail,
And saw me nevermore.

Perhaps she cast herself away
Lest both of us should drown:
Perhaps she feared to die, as they
Who die in Camden Town.

What came of her? The bitter nights
Destroy the rose and lily,
And souls are lost among the lights
Of painted Piccadilly.

What came of her? The river flows
So deep and wide and stilly,
And waits to catch the fallen rose
And clasp the broken lily.

I dream she dwells in London still
And breathes the evening air,
And often walk to Primrose Hill,
And hope to meet her there.

Once more together we will live,
For I will find her yet:
I have so little to forgive;
So much, I can't forget.

INDEX

Major quoted extracts are given after authors' names in bold type. Page references to biographical information about quoted authors appear in italics. Titles of quoted works are also rendered in italics.

ACKNOWLEDGEMENTS

Every effort has been made to contact the copyright holders of
material used. We would be pleased to hear from any copyright
owners we have been unable to reach to ensure that proper redress
is made and that due accreditation is given in future editions.
Thanks are due to all the authors and publishers who granted
permission to reproduce extracts from the following books:

Robert Hastings of Black Spring Press for permission to
reproduce the extract from Alexander Baron's *The Lowlife*;
The Andrew Lownie Literary Agency for *The Night Bathers* by
Julian Maclaren-Ross; HRH The Prince of Wales for permission
to reproduce a part of his Guildhall speech. The extract from *My
Autobiography* by Charles Chaplin, published by Bodley Head, is
reprinted by permission of the Random House Group Ltd.
Moonraker copyright © Glidrose Productions, 1955; text
reproduced with permission from Ian Fleming Publications Ltd.
Extract from *The War of the Worlds* reprinted with permission of
A.P. Watt Ltd on behalf of the Literary Executors of the Estate of
H.G. Wells. Thanks to Peter Owen Ltd, London, for permission to
reproduce the extract from Peter Vanisttart's *Landlord*. Extract
from Anthony Powell's *The Military Philosophers*, first published
1968 by William Heinemann Ltd, London, reprinted
with permission of David Higham Associates Ltd.

Cover image: Big Ben (detail) ©istockphoto.com/wrangel;
p. 6: ©istockphoto.com/Duncan Walker.